AKHENATEN AND TUTANKHAMUN
Revolution and Restoration

David P. Silverman
Josef W. Wegner
Jennifer Houser Wegner

University of Pennsylvania Museum of Archaeology and Anthropology, Philadelphia

Copyright © 2006 by the University of Pennsylvania Museum of Archaeology and Anthropology
3260 South Street
Philadelphia, PA 19104
USA

All Rights Reserved
First Edition

Cataloging-in-Publication data available from the U.S. Library of Congress
ISBN 1-931707-90-1

DAVID P. SILVERMAN is Curator, Egyptian Section, Penn Museum, and Eckley B. Coxe Professor of Egyptology, Department of Near Eastern Languages and Civilizations, University of Pennsylvania.

JOSEF W. WEGNER is Associate Curator, Egyptian Section, Penn Museum, and Associate Professor of Egyptian Archaeology, Department of Near Eastern Languages and Civilizations, University of Pennsylvania.

JENNIFER HOUSER WEGNER is Research Scientist, Egyptian Section, Penn Museum, and Adjunct Assistant Professor, Department of Near Eastern Languages and Civilizations, University of Pennsylvania.

All chapter epigraphs are from Murnane's 1995 translations of hieroglyphic texts from Amarna's boundary stelae.
Cover: Profile of the god Amun with features of Tutankhamun. Photograph courtesy of Charlie McMillan and Elizabeth Jean Walker.
Frontispiece: Statue of Amun. UPMAA E14350.

Manufactured in Canada on acid-free paper.

To our mothers

Gertrude Silverman
Kay Wegner
Peggy Houser

PUBLICATION OF THIS BOOK WAS MADE POSSIBLE BY THE GENEROSITY OF THE ANNENBERG FOUNDATION, WITH SPECIAL THANKS TO GREGORY ANNENBERG WEINGARTEN, TRUSTEE; AND OF SUSAN H. HORSEY.

Contents

Acknowledgments

This volume would not have come into being without the help of a substantial number of people, and we are grateful to each of them for all of the help they have given us.

Susan Horsey, a Member of the Penn Museum's Board of Overseers, has made the production of this book possible through her generosity and interest.

Gregory Annenberg Weingarten, also a member of the Penn Museum's Board of Overseers, has been a main supporter of both the publication and the accompanying exhibit, Amarna: Ancient Egypt's Place in the Sun, which opened in November 2006.

Dr. Richard M. Leventhal, the Williams Director of the Penn Museum, has been a constant source of encouragement throughout the project.

In the Egyptian Section, Elizabeth (Jean) Walker tirelessly photographed all of the objects, and many of the images appear in this book. Stephen Phillips assisted with scanning many of the slides to illustrate this book and compiling the bibliography and preparing the manuscript. Our section intern, Emily Toner, was instrumental in preparing the initial bibliography and producing preliminary drawings for many of the line art images.

We also want to thank many helpful and talented members of the Penn Museum community: Archives: Alex Pezzati, Alison Miner, and the Archives Staff; Conservation: Ginny Greene and Tom Fuller; Photo Studio: Francine Sarin and Jennifer Chiappardi; Publications: Walda Metcalf, Matt Manieri, Monica Mockus, Lauren Sankovitch, Minjoo Kweon, and Rachel Omansky; Education: Gillian Wakely; Our Project Manager, Klare Scarborough, was always there, keeping the wolves at bay while we completed the manuscript for the book.

Special thanks go to Tom Jenkins for his many photographs of Museum artifacts and to Dr. Robert K. Ritner of the University of Chicago who provided us with a number of his personal photographs from recent trips to the site of Amarna.

Chronology

Fig. 2. A view of the excavations of the Tomb of Tutankhamun, Valley of the Kings. Photographer Harry Burton recorded all aspects of the expedition after Howard Carter discovered the tomb in 1922.

memory eventually became better known in modern times than their detractor. Today Akhenaten and Tutankhamun are among the most celebrated pharaohs to have ruled Egypt.

Our knowledge of the events of the Amarna Period has resulted in large part from the richness of the archaeological discoveries made about them. After dismantling Akhenaten's temples, Horemheb recycled more than 100,000 blocks as filler for the core of his Karnak gateway, where they remained in darkness for thousands of years, hidden from the sunlight so important in Akhenaten's new religion. In the 1960s, a conservation project under the auspices of the Penn Museum exposed them, and their large number and good condition provided essential data about the reign of this

king. These blocks also supplemented contemporaneous records and other archaeological data about Akhenaten. Two factors affected the dearth of information about Tutankhamun: Horemheb's subsequent appropriation of his monuments and the young king's atypical burial in a hastily prepared tomb. Smaller than those of his ancestors, his tomb was located in a previously unused corner of the Valley of the Kings, where it remained hidden for more than 3,200 years. But the name of Tutankhamun resounds the loudest in the 20th century owing to the perseverance of the intrepid British archaeologist, Howard Carter (see Figure 160). When he discovered Tutankhamun's tomb and its fabulous treasure in 1922, the king's name reverberated around the world.

For nearly 75 years, scholars have debated much about Akhenaten and Tutankhamun. Considerable archaeological, iconographic, and textual information exists, but some of the information has more than one interpretation. For example, the exact

Fig. 3. Amarna blocks used as filler from Horemheb's Pylon in the Temple of Amun at Karnak. The Akhenaten Temple Project, begun in the 1960s under the auspices of the Penn Museum, recorded the blocks used as a core for the gateway that Horemheb built. Photograph courtesy of the Penn Akhenaten Temple Project.

parentage of Tutankhamun is not stated in texts. Was Akhenaten actually Tutankhamun's father, and if so, who was Tutankhamun's mother? How great an effect did his short 10-year reign have on his kingdom, and when did he begin his move south from the new capital at Amarna, in the middle of the country, back to the traditional city of Thebes? Did any of the Amarna kings serve in coregency? Who ascended the throne after Akhenaten and just prior to Tutankhamun? Was Akhenaten a visionary or a heretic? How successful were his policies of religious innovation, his concepts of kingship, and his manner of dealing with internal and external affairs? These are only some of the questions students of the period face.

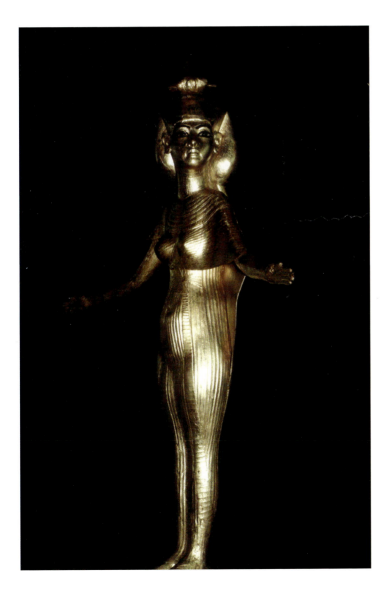

Fig. 4. Statue of the goddess Selket, from the Tomb of Tutankhamun. Selket's power was strong enough to cure the sting of a scorpion. She was also responsible for protecting the mummified intestines of Tutankhamun. Cairo Museum JE 60686. Photo courtesy of David P. Silverman. Gilded wood. Height 90 cm (35.4 in).

Fig. 5. Pectoral from the Tomb of Tutankhamun. The central element portrays a winged scarab referring to the sun god, with Thoth and Re-Horakhty, other traditional deities Tutankhamun restored, at the top. Cairo Museum JE 61884. Photo courtesy of David P. Silverman. Gold, silver, and semiprecious stones. Height 14.9 cm (5.9 in) and width 14.5 cm (5.7 in).

It is now clear that within a few generations after their deaths these two rulers had became nonentities in the eyes of their subjects. Those individuals in ancient Egypt who later composed the king lists—periodic registers of pharaohs who had reigned in prior times—omitted the names of the Amarna rulers. Akhenaten and Tutankhamun in effect ceased to exist, and their names and deeds faded from the collective memory.

Akhenaten had broken with tradition and replaced belief in many gods of the Egyptian pantheon with that in a single deity, the visible manifestation of the sun, the disk called Aten. He rejected Amun, the primary national deity since the 12th Dynasty (1938–1759 BCE) as well as his powerful priesthood, in favor of a new god for whom the king was the sole high priest. Acting swiftly, Akhenaten changed many aspects of society: religion, art, language, architecture, city planning, and concepts of kingship, to name a few. By the fifth year of his reign, or shortly thereafter, the king relocated the capital to a site without earlier settlement,

Fig. 6. Back of the "Ceremonial Chair" of Tutankhamun. The principal image in the center, the traditional god Heh, holds hieroglyphs signifying "a hundred thousand years" in each hand. The vignette represents the king's desire to reign for eternity. Cairo Museum JE 62028. Photo courtesy of David P. Silverman. Wood and sheet gold. Height 96 cm (37.8 in), width 47.6 cm (18.7 in), and depth 50.8 cm (20 in).

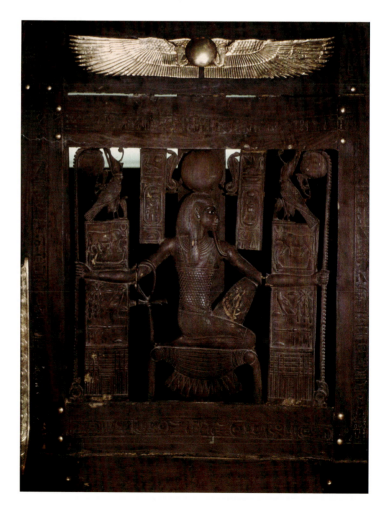

Fig. 7. Cartouches of Akhenaten. His throne name (Neferkheperure Waenre) appears on the left, and his altered birth name (Akhenaten) on the right. UPMAA E648. Limestone and pigment. Height 28 cm (11 in), width 30 cm (11.8 in), and depth 10 cm (3.9 in).

which he called Akhetaten "Horizon of the Aten," today known as Amarna.

For the population of this new city life centered on the king and his new god. It was here that a young prince was born around 1340 BCE. Named Tutankhaten—"Perfect is the Life of Aten"—he spent his early childhood in the royal court in Amarna and undoubtedly knew no other religion than Atenism. When Akhenaten died in 1336 BCE, the prince did not ascend the throne immediately, perhaps because of his age or rank. Two other members of the royal family may have ruled briefly, and it appears that they began the reconciliation with the gods of the pantheon that Akhenaten had rejected.

The traditional religion and the new religion coexisted for a time, and life at Akhetaten continued. When Tutankhaten began his rule, probably at about nine or ten years of age, he remained at Akhetaten, the only world he knew. He soon moved to Thebes and assumed the new name Tutankhamun—"Perfect is the life of

Amun"—marking his intentions to accept the former beliefs fully and to restore traditional ideology.

Despite Tutankhamun's actions to reinstate orthodox beliefs, he and those rulers associated with Akhenaten and his revolution eventually became reviled. Yet those doomed to oblivion by the ancient Egyptians are in modern times among the most renowned kings of the empire. This book will describe life during these times and how these two men affected the future of Egypt.

Fig.8, opposite. Statue of Tutankhamun from his tomb. This figure is rendered in the naturalistic style introduced during the Amarna Period. It depicts the king wearing the Red Crown of Lower Egypt. Cairo Museum JE 60709. Photo courtesy of David P. Silverman. Wood and gilt. Height 69.5 cm (27.4 in).

1

THE EVOLUTION OF THE PHARAOH AKHENATEN

The Sole One of the Sun-God

During the 2nd millennium BCE, several powerful nation states competed with each other for dominance in the areas of North Africa, Mediterranean Europe, and western Asia. Since each had different religions, languages, and customs, communication among them was often complicated. Although they engaged in international trade and diplomacy, competition led to frequent battles, and soon a few superpowers emerged in the ancient Near East. None, however, could boast the longevity of Egypt's civilization.

One of most powerful Egyptian pharaohs, Tuthmosis III (1479-1425 BCE), rose to the throne during the 18th Dynasty (1539-1292 BCE) and led his nation to many victories. He established an extensive empire whose borders went beyond the limits that his predecessors had set. Successors maintained the advances he had made, but they also achieved their own victories. Direct inheritance allowed several generations of the Tuthmosid line to control the throne without interruption, and the usually peaceful transition of power and consistent governmental agendas ensured prosperity.

By the time Amenhotep III (1390-1353 BCE) received his crown, just prior to his teen years (not much older than his probable grandson, Tutankhamun, some 58 years later), Egypt had firmly established itself as a dominant power. While this pharaoh eventually had to engage in military activity to retain his control of vassal states and to maintain security in border areas, he had a long and relatively calm reign. Internal and external peace allowed him to give attention to a variety of cultural activities, and he brought the art of diplomacy to new heights. His primary wife, Queen Tiye, with whom he shared power, was of noble, not royal, blood. Like many other royal women of the period who preceded her, she had a very strong character and played a significant role during her husband's reign. Under the rule of this powerful couple, art, architecture, and literature thrived, and this period in Egypt's history often is described as a "golden age."

On the throne for almost four decades, Amenhotep III took interest in exploring the possible modification of aspects of royal ideology and religious doctrine. Why he wanted to alter beliefs that

had already been in place for more than 1,500 years is not clear. Perhaps his political acumen warned him that change might be necessary in order to preserve pharaonic power. He might have seen the growing influence and wealth of the priesthood of the god Amun as potential competition for the throne. Indeed, such a struggle between pharaoh and the high priest of Amun eventually occurred at the end of the 20th Dynasty. Perhaps the king had an inquisitive mind or a philosophical disposition. Whatever the reasons, he began to make subtle changes in royal ideology, promoting the concept of a divine living king and related religious beliefs. Eventually, he made his intentions explicit when he erected cult places around the country in which he could be worshipped as a living god, thus expanding the prevailing concept of kingship.

He also decreed that a series of scenes be carved on the walls of the state Temple of Amun at Luxor, recording his divine birth with this god designated as his father. Earlier in the dynasty, Queen Hatshepsut had used similar iconography, but she limited her imagery in large part to placement in a funerary temple. In the mortuary monument that she built at Deir el-Bahri, she established a cult for her worship as a divinity after death. It appears that she did break with the tradition of using only such monuments for this type of iconography when she had scenes reflecting her divine birth carved in her chapel at the state temple at Karnak.

Amenhotep III expanded on her actions. He placed the text and image proclaiming his divine status on the walls of a "birth" chapel he constructed in the Temple of Amun Re at Luxor, a building used for ongoing rituals during the lifetime of the king. Amenhotep thus introduced and publicly emphasized a new concept, that of a divine living king. This temple served as the place for ritual and sometimes-actual coronation, thus visibly relating divine birth to ascension to the throne. In more subtle ways, he also brought special prominence to the sun god Re, even using the epithet "dazzling disk of the sun" to refer to himself. This royal phrase identified the king with a visible manifestation of the sun, the Aten "disk." This term had appeared only sporadically in earlier periods, but under this pharaoh, the sun's disk began to receive more attention, especially regarding the king. The importance of this move would become apparent within a few years.

His presumed second son Amenhotep IV (1353-1336) inherited this privileged but changing environment when he began his rule. Already an adult at his accession to the throne, he succeeded his father, probably without coregency. His transition to the throne seemed seamless. Like his father, Amenhotep IV married an influential woman from a nonroyal family. The legendary beauty of his queen, Nefertiti, has filtered down into our own times, based in large part on the magnificent sculptor's painted model, now in Berlin, that was excavated in the new capital city at Amarna (ancient Akhetaten) built by her husband.

Fig. 9, opposite. Sculpted head of Tuthmosis III. Known as the "Napoleon of Ancient Egypt" for his military prowess, young Tuthmosis III began his reign under the regency of his aunt, the female Pharaoh Hatshepsut. Credited with founding Egypt's empire, he wears the crown of Upper Egypt with a protective *uraeus* (cobra) at his brow. UPMAA E14370. Red granite. Height 53.3 (21 in), width 25.39 cm (10 in), and depth 40.63 cm (16 in.)

Fig. 10. Seal of Amenhotep III. An inscription with the king's name and titles appears on the bottom of the seal. The image above depicts a prostrate king praying to the creator god Atum, whose name is inscribed between the pharaoh's hands. UP-MAA 48.16.1. Steatite. Height 2.2 cm (.9 in), width 1 cm (.4 in), and length 6.3 cm (2.5 in).

Fig. 11. The inscription on the base of the seal of Amenhotep III lists both the king's throne name and his birth name in cartouches. It also records some of his titles and epithets: "The Good God, Lord of the Two Lands, Nebmaatre, Son of Re, Amenhotep, Ruler of Thebes." UPMAA 48.16.1. Steatite. Height 2.2 cm (.9 in), width 1 cm (.4 in), and length 6.3 cm (2.5 in).

His devotion to her and her importance to him is evident in the prominence she plays in temple iconography, even in the early Theban temples. She wears a unique tall crown and appears with her husband more than any other royal wife. She even takes on roles primarily reserved for pharaohs, for example, in the pose of striking down enemies. The mother of six daughters, she appears in many reliefs, paintings, and sculptures. Apparently she bore no sons. By tradition, prior to the Ramesside Period princes do not appear in royal scenes. So, if she had borne the young prince Tutankhaten (later called Tutankhamun), his image would not have accompanied any of those of his female siblings.

In the very earliest years of his reign at Thebes, Amenhotep IV appeared to respect the deep-seated traditions already in place for more than a millennium, but even then he had begun to reveal elements of his intensely personal devotion to the sun god. The solar religion had always remained an important aspect of ancient Egyptian beliefs, but in the 18th Dynasty it received a new prominence. Now, Amenhotep IV went further. Emphasis first appeared in the descriptive phrases he devised for this deity, which suggested universality and immanence.

Fig. 12. Colossal statues of Queen Tiye and Amenhotep III. Cairo Museum CG 610. These royal figures are the same scale and size, indicating the important position the queen enjoyed during her husband's reign. Photo courtesy of David P. Silverman. Limestone. Height 7 m (275.6 in) and width 4 m (157.5 in).

He focused on Re-Horakhty, an aspect of the solar god, and associated him with new iconography that portrayed the disk of the sun with anthropomorphized rays descending toward the earth. Still at Thebes in the fifth year of his reign, he had set in place many innovations in religious iconography and phraseology. New pharaohs often began their reigns constructing temples, and while Amenhotep IV followed suit, his builders utilized new techniques. They employed smaller building blocks that allowed for quicker construction. Royal statuary typically stood in front of temples, but the colossal figures this pharaoh's sculptors created portrayed the king in a radical style showing unusual proportions, exaggerated features, and elongated and swollen limbs. This unorthodox appearance caused some scholars to suggest that the king was being depicted as a male/female primordial creator deity. No inscriptional evidence accompanies these figures to support such a conclusion, and throughout Egypt's history, only male creator gods were portrayed.

Sculptors utilized the new style for representations of royal and nonroyal figures in two dimensions on the reliefs decorating the walls of the temples. Given the extent of its use, this mannered style, with more fluid lines and an emphasis on the curvilinear aspects rather than angularity of the body and gestures, may have been an attempt to conform to the emphasis on the natural world that was a hallmark of the king's ideology. His artists frequently used floral motifs with flexible stems, and they portrayed the human figure in more relaxed positions, often bending over. Intimate

Fig. 13, opposite. Statuette of Amun. This powerful state god wears a false beard, pleated kilt, and double-feathered crown. Perhaps originally painted and gilded, this figure is a relatively rare example of Amun carved in wood. UPMAA E14325. Wood. Height 21.5 cm (8.5 in), width 3.7 cm (1.5 in), and depth 3.2 cm (1.3 in).

Fig. 14. Temple of Amun at Luxor. Beyond the gateway constructed by Ramses II lie parts of the temple built by earlier pharaohs, including a chamber of Amenhotep III in which divine birth scenes were carved. Photo courtesy of David P. Silverman.

Fig. 15. Temple of Hatshepsut at Deir el Bahri, Thebes. The female Pharaoh Hatshepsut modeled her mortuary structure on the adjacent temple of the earlier ruler Mentuhotep II. Constructed in a series of terraces below the peak of the mountain, it has scenes of her divine birth carved on the walls of one area. Photo courtesy of David P. Silverman.

scenes involving the members of the royal family appear for the first time. Using sunk relief, a quicker method than raised relief, the artisans carved rather deeply, so the curved lines they now favored would appear especially emphasized when the raking light of the sun shone on the surface of the wall and imbued the figure with a new vitality.

The speed with which the king moved while still at Thebes seems to imply how driven he was to have his new ideas quickly become dogma. He may have reasoned that swift action would deny time for negative reaction, and thus prevent rebellion.

In the midst of all of this activity and the upheaval that must have resulted from the actual move after his fifth year of more

Fig. 16. Sculptor's model relief of Akhenaten's profile. Within a few years after Akhenaten ascended the throne, his sculptors depicted all human figures with exaggerated features. These details became more naturalistic a bit later, and the slightly elongated facial elements in this relief suggest a date just after the early part of the king's reign. UPMAA 856. Limestone. Height 21.5 cm (8.5 in) and width 19.5 cm (7.7 in).

than 20,000 people to Akhetaten, the pharaoh also changed his name. At birth he had received the name Amenhotep IV, which included the designation of the traditional god Amun: "Amun is satisfied." Since the king now intended to suppress this deity along with others in the pantheon in favor of his new god, the Aten, he chose to call himself Akhenaten: "The One Beneficial/Effective for the Aten."

During this same short period of time, he had begun working on his plans to establish a new capital city. He found a perfect site at a location in Middle Egypt. Situated on the east bank of the Nile, it was territory sacred to no other god. At the eastern edge of the city lay cliffs separated by a valley. This specific landscape may have impressed Akhenaten greatly, for the U-shaped bay between the cliffs, with the dried riverbed through it, formed the ancient Egyptian hieroglyph meaning "horizon"— *akhet*. Moreover, at sunrise, with the sun's disk, the A*ten*, low in the sky and positioned in the center of this "natural horizon," the image literally spelled out *Akhet-aten*, meaning "the horizon of the sun disk." He chose this site for his new city, and he called it Akhetaten (modern Amarna). For the Egyptians the *akhet* was the region where the sun god emerged from the darkness of the night (the D*uat*) and was reborn each day. Thus the Aten in the horizon, Akhetaten, symbolically represented the continually regenerating cosmos.

With the construction of temples in a new style, the formulation of plans to build a new capital city, the introduction of an original style of art, the shift from the emphasis on the traditional pantheon

Fig. 17. Bust of Queen Nefertiti. Excavators discovered this painted sculpture of Akhenaten's favorite wife in the house of the Sculptor Tuthmosis at Amarna. Its form and "blind" eye suggest that it functioned as an artist's model. Ägyptisches Museum 21 217. Berlin. Photo courtesy of David P. Silverman. Limestone and pigment. Height 48 cm (18.9 in).

of gods to a radical ideology with a focus on the sun god, his reorganization of the bureaucracy and restructuring of the priesthood with those loyal to him in power, and organizing and moving some 20,000 people to a new city still in the construction stage, Akhenaten was clearly a very busy individual in the early years of his reign.

Correspondence with other nations during his reign suggests that while maintaining relations with foreign states, he may have paid less attention to international diplomacy than his father had. His interests focused more on his theological changes, yet he managed to retain much of Egypt's status and reputation. Records on Egyptian monuments show scant evidence of a strong presence in military affairs, although he did oversee several campaigns and maintained full control over the army. It is important to note that without the army's support, Akhenaten could not have instituted all of the changes he made. It appears that he preferred to remain in Akhetaten. There, however, he was not a continuously visible ruler to the majority of the population who lived outside the new capital, as pharaohs had been in the past. Still, monuments to the new god appear outside Akhetaten, signifying the pharaoh's influence throughout Egypt.

In addition to his other modifications, he began making significant changes to the formal language that appeared on his monuments, changes especially clear at Amarna. Hieroglyphic texts had previously followed a classical model called Middle Egyptian, but the texts included selected elements of the vernacular language, which quickly appeared with regularity. This mixed form of expres-

Fig. 18. View toward Akhetaten (modern Amarna). The focus of the landscape of Akhenaten's new capital was the natural indentation in the eastern cliffs which formed the hieroglyph *akhet* "horizon." When the sun rose within, it physically represented Akhetaten, "The Horizon of the Sun Disk." Photo courtesy of David P. Silverman.

Fig. 19. Relief from the Amarna tomb of Panehesy. The Chief Servitor of the Aten and the Second Prophet, Panehesy was an important official in Akhenaten's court. He also held the title of Overseer of the Granary and Cattle of the Aten. Texts composed using the new grammar appear before him. Amarna. Photo courtesy of David P. Silverman.

sion represented a style unique to Akhenaten and, like the art and other aspects of his program, it, too, centered on the king himself.

While other kings before him had altered their names and moved their capital cities, introducing new styles of art and innovative architectural techniques, none had gone to such extremes. We may never know what motivated Akhenaten, but no one would contest the dedication he had to his ideas. His commitment resulted in a cultural experiment that had no precedent in Egypt. What was the basis? What were the goals? What succeeded and what failed? The answers to these questions can help us understand whether Akhenaten was a philosopher, a madman, or a prophet.

2

The Religion of the Aten

Praise to You, O Aten, When You Arise to Illuminate Every Land with Your Beauty

Akhenaten's new religion appears drastically different from the beliefs the Egyptians had already followed for many centuries. Traditional doctrines had centered on a pantheon filled with a variety of gods. Some functioned in one or several of the following areas: funerary, national, local, personal, household, and foreign. Others had associations with natural phenomenon, abstract concepts, and human qualities and emotions. The form they took varied as well. Gods and goddesses could appear as a human, an animal, or a combination of both. Rarely did the Egyptians envision their deities as fantastic creatures with features not observable in nature.

The king, while clearly identified as a god after death, took the role of intermediary between humankind and the deities during his life on earth. He held the position of high priest of every god, at least in theory. As he underwent the ritual of coronation, he received the title of "son of Re" (the sun god) that would appear in the list of titles and epithets that precede his birth name. This designation would affirm his status as divine progeny. He then assumed the divine throne of the god Horus. He also received a second, or "throne" name, preceded by the designation, "King of Upper and Lower Egypt," a reference to the division of the land in its earlier history and his role as a unifier. Once in position as pharaoh, the new ruler became identified with the divine eternal office that had existed since the first ruler had assumed the throne of a unified land prior to 3100 BCE. Achieving a state of true divinity, however, came to him only after death, burial, ritual, and transformation. Until then, he ranked below the gods, whose superhuman powers, omniscience, and omnipotence he did not possess.

Akhenaten's predecessors had ruled their country with varying degrees of power, and it is interesting to see how later generations perceived their pharaohs. Literary sources from the Middle Kingdom (1980-1630 BCE) refer back to specific kings from the Old Kingdom, sometimes with praises, sometimes with criticism. Although texts from the Amarna Period concentrate on the new

theology and do not contain such direct references, Akhenaten was certainly aware of the past. His focus on aspects of the solar god may have arisen out of familiarity with the teachings of the influential priesthood of Re at Heliopolis. The 18th Dynasty had seen renewed focus on the solar cult and the introduction of new sun hymns. The time when this cult was at its height, however, was the age of the pyramids, and these monuments might have served as inspiration for him.

Egypt of the 4th Dynasty was seen not only as a magnificent period, with colossal structures at sites such as Giza, Saqqara, and Abusir; it was also a time when the glory of both the sun god and his representative on earth, the pharaoh, were at a peak. The patriarchal relationship between Re and the new king is an important part of the theology in the 4th Dynasty, and during this period, the title "Son of Re" first appeared joined with the car-

Fig. 20, opposite. Statue of Sekhmet. A goddess with combative traits, Sekhmet was thought to have the power to send plagues and other diseases against enemies through her fiery arrows. Her images often accompanied the pharaoh on military activities, and the Egyptians also invoked her to ward off or cure diseases. This figure is one of the less-common standing types; others are seated. UPMAA E2049. Granodiorite. Height 86.4 cm (34 in), width 45.7 cm (18 in), and depth 48.3 cm (19 in).

Fig. 21. Plaque of Bes. Nine monkeys on one side of this two-sided charm surround Bes. A god of fertility and sexuality, with leonine face and dwarflike limbs, he also protected mothers and children. UPMAA E14358. Faience. Height 21.5 cm (8.5 in), width 7.7 cm (3 in), and depth 2.7 cm (1.1 in).

touche, an oval ring that encircled the name of the king, bearing the royal birth name. Akhenaten may have longed to recreate in some way that idealized royal state, a time when the solar god had enjoyed its supreme power and its patriarchal relationship with the king first came into existence. Perhaps for this reason he constructed monuments in the Memphite area and in Heliopolis early in his reign, and he continued to have interest in these areas later as well.

If Akhenaten was aware of such developments in earlier times, he may have understood his father's steps to set up his own divinity on earth as a move parallel to the situation in the 4th Dynasty when pharaoh and Re had become preeminent. While Amenhotep III had explicitly identified himself with the god Amun in the scenes of his divine birth in the temple of that god in Luxor, not the sun god, he also had identified with aspects of Re, calling himself the dazzling disk of the sun. In this latter action, perhaps Amenhotep III had also conceived of himself as one with the solar deity.

His son, Akhenaten, appears to have accepted the concept his father had put forth. Then, when he ascended the throne, he may have considered himself the literal son of Re, the son god (now personified by his father) and a visible living embodiment of his newly acquired title designating him as such, s3 R'(son of Re) (see Figure 23).

He therefore did not need to claim divinity from Amun, whose name means "the Hidden One"; his sire was Amenhotep III, the "dazzling disk of the Aten," a very evident aspect of the sun itself. He added the phrase "may my father live" before the name of his new god.

This strong identification with Amenhotep III and the belief in the divinity of his father may have prompted the son to celebrate

Fig. 22, opposite. Figure of Ptah. The patron of artisans as well as a creator god, Ptah wears his characteristic apparel—a skullcap, a close-fitting garment, and a false beard. He holds a staff combining the hieroglyphic symbols for "life," "stability," and "dominion"—*ankh, djed,* and *was*. UPMAA E14294. Bronze. Height 25 cm (9 in), width 10.15 cm (4 in), and depth 7.6 cm (3 in).

Fig. 23. Cartouches of Ramses III from Medinet Habu. Carved and painted, this inscription above a doorway in the mortuary temple of Ramses III records a wish that is read in both directions from a central *ankh*: 1 (from right to left) "May the Son of Re, Ramses, The ruler of Heliopolis [his birth name], live" and 2 (from left to right) "May the Good God, Usermaatre-setepenre [his throne name], live." Medinet Habu, Thebes. Photo courtesy of David P. Silverman.

Fig. 24. Titulary of Tuthmosis III from Deir el Bahri. This inscription from the mortuary temple records the king's birth name, Tuthmosis, and his throne name, Menkheperre, in cartouches. It also lists several royal titles and epithets that Tuthmosis III received at his coronation, among which are Horus, Strong Bull, King of Upper and Lower Egypt, and Son of Re. Deir el Bahri, Thebes. Photo courtesy of David P. Silverman.

a first *heb-sed* festival uncharacteristically early, in the second or third year of his reign. This celebration of royal jubilee, marking rejuvenation, traditionally occurred after the thirtieth year of a pharaoh's reign, and then at shorter intervals thereafter. For some scholars, Akhenaten's timing of this event was deliberate, for it coincided with what would have been the fortieth year of his father's reign, the appropriate time for a fourth festival to take place for him. At this time the first texts that refer to a jubilee for the sun disk appear. This event is important, as it suggests that the new king was poised to begin a unique chapter in Egypt's history. By referring to the jubilee of a god, a festival reserved previously for royalty, Akhenaten was assigning royal attributes to a deity. Still in the early years of his reign and calling himself Amenhotep IV, his actual birth name, the king had simultaneously accepted and expanded the concept of divine kingship and had adjusted the status of deities. Thus he began his program to equalize royal and divine status.

Amenhotep IV reconsidered the traditional understanding of kingship and divinity. He followed a holistic path, using language, art, philosophy, architecture, and the environment to promote his ideology. Some see in his actions a synchronized elevation of the position of pharaoh and a lowering of that of the god. In addition to jubilees, the Aten now had cartouches surrounding its name, devices previously used only for kings and queens. Aten, the sun disk, now bore the *uraeus* (cobra) just as did royalty. Prayers of offering invoked both the king and the Aten; certain epithets were shared; and year dates on inscriptions included the name of Akhenaten and his god.

While earlier kings functioned as the high priest of each of the gods, for reasons of practicality actual priests, whose titles designated their specific service, often took the monarch's place in temples throughout the land. Akhenaten now functioned as the sole high priest of the Aten, and he required his own high priest. This modification in the structure of the priesthood also had the benefit of insuring clerical loyalty to pharaoh.

Fig. 25. The pyramid and sphinx of Khafre. A human-headed lion, the sphinx bears the face of the 4th Dynasty ruler Khafre, whose pyramid rises in the background. Both stuctures relate to the solar cult. More than a thousand years later, pharaohs of the 18th Dynasty built temples and monuments here indicating the continued importance of this cult. Giza. Photo courtesy of David P. Silverman.

Fig. 26. *Heb-sed* relief. The shape of this block is similar to that of a talatat, the type of block used in Akhenaten's buildings. This part of the relief depicts the pharaoh in festival garb, as he celebrates the royal *Heb-sed* ritual. Fitzwilliam Museum EGA 2300.1943. Photo courtesy of David P. Silverman. Limestone. Height 23 cm (9.0 inches), width 53 cm (20.8 inches), and depth 6.5 cm (2.4 inches)

While people in the past could pray directly to their personal gods and worship other deities during festival time, they no longer had such access in this exclusive religion. Depictions on temple walls and stelae show only the king and queen worshiping before the disk of the sun. The Aten's rays, ending in human hands, formed the only visible anthropomorphic element of the new god. They extended down only toward the royal family, concentrating on the king and queen. The *ankh*, "life," they offered went solely to Akhenaten, sometimes to his wife, but not to the princesses who often appeared in the scene. Vignettes carved on the walls in the tombs of the elite in the capital city Amarna depict the subjects generally bowing before the king, a distance away from the disk and its rays.

Pharaoh now used for himself the description *ankh m maat*, "living on maat (cosmic order, balance, and decorum)." In the past this phrase referred primarily to deities. In orthodox beliefs, gods had family groupings, often consisting of a father, mother, and offspring. The Aten, however, was a universal creator deity with no divine consort or offspring: Akhenaten and his family took their place. It is also conceivable that Akhenaten, Nefertiti, the six princesses, and the Aten together represented a parallel to the traditional ennead, a group of nine gods in the Heliopolitan creation myth centered in the city of Heliopolis in the north. This theology of cosmic evolution was one of Egypt's earliest, and one that clearly influenced Akhenaten.

During festivals priests now carried on their shoulders Akhenaten and Nefertiti seated in chairs. The priests formerly bore statues of gods in shrines on their shoulders as they displayed them to the people. Under Akhenaten's rule, only two-

Fig. 27. Fragment of a relief. During the reign of Akhenaten, his sole god, the Aten, received cartouches, previously a royal prerogative. The ovals appear here on the side of a table of offerings and contain the earlier name and epithets of the Aten: "The living one, Re-Horus of the two horizons who rejoices in the horizon in his name being 'Illumination-which-is-in-the-solar-disk.'" UPMAA E857. Amarna. Quartzite. Height 22 cm (8.7 in), width 14 cm (5.5 cm), and depth 7.3 cm (2.9 in).

dimensional depictions of the disk existed, its only human element being the hands at the ends of the sun's rays. Sculptors created no three-dimensional representations of the disk, as the king himself was now the living embodiment of the deity. In the new doctrine the god was visible on earth in human form and in the sky as a golden disk.

For his dogma and the glory of his deity, the Aten, Akhenaten required new territory. He founded Amarna, almost 200 miles north of Thebes, and soon closed the door on pantheism in ancient Egypt, vowing never to leave the area, although his texts contain the caveat that should he die outside Amarna, his burial should take place there. Some scholars feel that he acted for political reasons, primarily to stem the rising powers of the wealthy priesthood of Amun, and this developing situation may well have influenced both his father and him. Indeed, by the end of the 20th Dynasty, the last Ramesside rulers, a series of kings of the New Kingdom bearing the name Ramesses, had become weak, and the priesthood of Amun based at Thebes had become so powerful that by the following dynasty it effectively ruled from the south. Did Akhenaten foresee such a possibility and was it a motivation in his radical changes? It is impossible to say for certain, but it is clear that the closure of the traditional temples, the establishment of a new line of priests loyal to him, and the move to a new capital at Amarna reinforced his control of the monarchy.

The nature of the individual undoubtedly motivated Akhenaten, for his passion, vigor, and resolve were unprecedented. He appears driven, almost a visionary. In record time he composed new hymns to reflect his new beliefs; he devised innovative types of architecture in which to worship his deity; and he developed original styles of art, as well as specific iconography, liturgy, and prayers. To ensure the suppression of the traditional gods Akhenaten eventually ordered all activity in temples of traditional

Fig. 28. Part of a relief. This fragment preserves the lower part of the Aten with the *uraeus*, another previously royal prerogative, at its base. Solar rays project downward, and a small portion of an arm, upraised in offering, remains intact. Only one of the Egyptian alabaster cartouches survives, enclosing the latter part of the Aten's name: "in his name being 'Illumination-which- is-in-the-solar-disk.'" UPMAA E2204a. Amarna. Calcite. Height 15 cm (5.9 in), width 13 cm (5.1 in), depth 11.5 cm (4.5 in).

gods to cease. Sometime after the 9th year of his reign, he sent agents to hack out the names of all deities from every text. He also commanded them to remove the plural element in the word "gods."

While Aten was the center of the religion and Amarna its sacred site, the king constructed temples, kiosks, and shrines in other parts of the country, as well. Some predated the move, but a few appear to have been contemporaneous with it. While only a small portion of Egypt's population of perhaps 3,000,000 people emigrated with the king, he ruled from Akhetaten with a considerable measure of power. His subjects beyond the boundaries of this city

Fig. 29. Fragment with text and relief. Several figures, some of whom wear the so-called Nubian wig, bend forward in a gesture of obeisance, presumably in honor of the king. The Aten, no longer preserved, must have appeared at the top of the scenes, and the remaining text mentions its rays. Ägyptisches Museum. Berlin. Photo courtesy of David P. Silverman.

probably never saw him, since he had decreed that he would never leave, and his ritual appearances took place only in Amarna. This lack of royal visibility may have enabled them to maintain earlier beliefs.

Archaeological evidence has revealed that even in the new capital people did not accept the radical ideology fully. The presence of small figures of traditional gods, as well as molds for the production of amulets in their forms, suggest that, despite the speed, extent, energy, and dedication with which Akhenaten installed and promoted his beliefs, he was unable to force his subjects to break entirely with tradition. The significant number of these items that have survived indicate that their production continued throughout the Amarna occupation.

Akhenaten's hymns tell the story of the world as he envisioned it. He had put his thoughts, beliefs, and ideology into texts, and they explain a world concentrating on the element of light embodied in the disk of the sun. The disk became a symbol of universality; it meant eternal light, harmony, and beauty; it was also the unique creator of the cosmos. This new god was described as the sole unique one, before whom there was no other. Darkness, and what occurred during it, was minimized and not explained in detail, while creation and recreation, with the emergence of the morning sun, was emphasized. He even planned his burial location in the eastern cliffs which formed the *akhet* (horizon) of *Akhetaten* (Amarna). Rather than in the traditional locations of the past on the west side of the Nile, he could be reborn every day with the sun in the eastern horizon. As a universal cosmic doctrine, Atenism encompassed the visible and perceived world, but it did not treat all elements within it

Fig. 30, opposite. Statue of Isis and Horus. The small figure of Horus, son of Osiris and Isis, sits nursing on the lap of his mother. He wears the sidelock of youth and has the *uraeus* of royalty on his brow. UPMAA E12548. Bronze. Height 40.8 cm (16.1 in), width 10.7 cm (4.2 in), and depth 15.49cm (6.1 in).

Fig. 31. Relief depicting the royal family of Amarna. Akhenaten and Nefertiti sit below the focus of the new religion, the Aten. They seem quite involved with their three daughters, one of whom plays with her mother's earring. The rays of the sun's disk end in human hands, some of which offer ankh "life" to the nostrils of the king and queen only. Ägyptisches Museum 14145. Berlin. Photo courtesy of David P. Silverman. Limestone. Height 33 cm (13 in), width 39 cm (15.4 in), and depth 3.8 cm (1.5 in).

equally; it concentrated on animate rather than inanimate elements, day rather than night, tended to stress the positive, and was rarely pessimistic.

While the hymns portray the beauty of the sun, the magnificence of its creations, and the life forms that derive from it, they avoid the specifics about just how all of this takes place. Earlier ideology used mythology replete with gods and goddesses to explain cosmic events. Doctrines also explained in detail death, how to prepare for the afterlife, and the dangers to be found in the underworld. In other words, the basic eschatology so important in Egyptian beliefs of the past no longer had a significant role. Although Akhenaten apparently constructed a kiosk to Osiris at Abydos fairly early in his reign, he soon shunned this deity, the myths associated with him, and all funerary deities. Mortuary literature and paraphernalia were avoided and only funerary figurines without the traditional *shabti* spell from the Book of the Dead persisted. Previously, these Osiride figurines, which were meant to perform forced labor in the afterlife, carried inscriptions on their surface to ensure their participation when called to action. Now, they had only the names and the titles of the deceased. Death had become more like sleep, with the new day bringing recreation. It was no longer a transition during which one proved him/herself worthy of an afterlife.

He proscribed other gods, as well as the explanatory myths surrounding them, once he had established himself fully at Amarna. His new capital had become appropriate only for the new form of deity he had devised and the unique type of pharaoh he had become.

The Egypt he conceived of and created differed decidedly from that of his ancestors and to a great extent ignored reality. While aspects of his god and the new concept of kingship had roots in the

Fig. 32, opposite. Stelophorous statue. Hednakht, an official of the 18th Dynasty, probably commissioned this statue for placement within a temple environment, as an exhibition of his piety. Kneeling behind a stela displaying a hymn to the sun god, Hednakht raises his hands in adoration to the solar deity. During the later Amarna Period, followers of Akhenaten may have deliberately damaged the names of deities in the fourth line, as part of the royal order to remove the names of the traditional gods from monuments. UPMAA L.55.212. Limestone and pigment. Height 35.55 cm (14 in), width 13.96 cm (5.5 in), depth 20.32 cm (8 in).

Fig. 33. Relief from tomb. This relief appears to have come from the Saqqara tomb of Merneith, an 18th Dynasty official, whose career spanned much of the Amarna Period. Agents dispersed throughout the kingdom some time around Year 9 of Akhenaten's reign were to remove the names of traditional gods from monuments. In this case, they altered the tomb owner's name from Merneith, with a reference to Neith, a goddess of the orthodoxy, to Meritire, with a reference to Re, the solar god. While they successfully "corrected" two instances of the name, they missed the first occurrence. The original name, Merneith, still stands at the bottom of the first and the top of the second line. Ägyptisches Museum 2070. Berlin. Photo courtesy of David P. Silverman.

past, significant components were alien to fundamental Egyptian principles. Maat, cosmic order, was so important to the Egyptians that they deified it as a goddess. Akhenaten, who avoided naming other deities, retained this concept and included it in texts at Amarna, emphasizing that he lived according to its principles. The inscriptions where this word appears do not always use the hieroglyph denoting divinity after it, suggesting that while the concept of maat endured, its divine status was perhaps being phased out.

Akhenaten may have envisioned life, the environment, and the surroundings in his new city as a paradise, and he unambiguously records it as such in his texts, but harsh reality intruded from all sides. A diplomatic letter from Ashuruballit I, ruler of Assyria, lamented the fate of emissaries who were forced to stand for hours in the blazing sun in a roofless reception area. This ruler mocked Akhenaten, noting that if the pharaoh wished to stand in the blazing sun, it was fine, but others would die from the exposure. While Akhenaten may have understood this exposure to the sun in his

Fig. 34. Molds of traditional gods. Casts made from these molds would have produced amulets in the form of the domestic deities, Bes (the four on the bottom) and Taweret (on the top). While the religion of the Amarna Period suppressed traditional beliefs, worship of the old gods persisted, even in the new capital, Amarna. UPMAA E726, E680, E733, E686 and E678a. Pottery. Heights range from 2.5 cm (1 in) to 4 cm (1.6 in).

Fig. 35. Amarna tomb scene depicting the funeral of Akhenaten's second daughter, Princess Meketaten. The royal family stands grieving to the right of the deceased daughter. Accompanying them on two registers to the right are female mourners, some of whom also raise their arms to their heads in gestures of bereavement. After Martin (1989b: pl. 68).

new roofless buildings as an introduction to the new god, it was in reality an action that could easily lead to death.

As Akhenaten's ideology became more extreme, the Egyptians began to see their new god-king less as a divinity and more as an individual with very human weaknesses. They also came to realize that the regime had ushered in a faltering economy. Enemies from Asia were encroaching, and the pharaoh's leadership was clearly failing. When one of Akhenaten's daughters died his subjects became aware that their king could suffer from some of the same human problems as they. Her tomb had depictions of a very human grieving family. As the reality of what was actually happening around them locally, nationally, and internationally manifested itself among the people, those in higher positions in Amarna concluded that Akhenaten's experiment in which they were participating had not succeeded. Egypt needed new leadership.

3

FOUNDING AKHENATEN'S CAPITAL CITY

May His Lordship Govern from Akhetaten

In the artwork and texts of the Amarna Period Akhenaten repeatedly emphasizes that he has a unique relationship with "his father," the Aten. The ultimate expression of Akhenaten's veneration of his single god occurred early in his reign when the king chose to establish a new capital city dedicated to the worship of the Aten. This city would serve as the heart of a newly fashioned Egypt ruled over by the sun disk with Akhenaten as the divinely sanctioned king who alone understood the true nature of the Aten.

The remains of this city, the site now called Tell el-Amarna (or simply Amarna), provides the bulk of the evidence for understanding Akhenaten's reign and its aftermath. The city's ruins occupy a vast desert bay, approximately 4 miles long and 2 miles wide, on the eastern side of the Nile. Equidistant between Memphis and Thebes, Amarna had an advantageous position in the center of Egypt. The king chose its location, however, not because of its geography, but through a form of divine inspiration.

Akhenaten's decision to establish a new royal city was not unprecedented. Egypt's first historical capital, Memphis, was founded at the beginning of Dynasty I (ca. 3000 BCE) as the royal residence of *Ineb-Hedj*, the "White-Wall." Similarly, Amenemhat I, first ruler of Dynasty 12, founded a capital named *Itjet-Tawy* near the Fayum region which served as the seat of Egypt's pharaohs during the Middle Kingdom (ca. 1950-1700 BCE). Forty years after the death of Akhenaten, Ramses II established his own capital city in the Delta, named *Per-Ramesse*, the "House-of-Ramses." What makes Akhenaten's city unique among these other royal capitals is that in choosing its location, the king's inspiration was explicitly religious rather than political, economic, or strategic in character.

We know a considerable amount about Amarna's founding from the preservation of a series of official boundary stelae—13 in all are known—ringing the perimeter of the city. Cut into the cliffs on both sides of the Nile (ten on the eastern side, three on the west), these boundary stelae have scenes, and in some cases engaged statues, of Akhenaten, Nefertiti, and their three eldest daughters (Meritaten, Meketaten, and Ankhesenpaaten) worshipping the Aten.

The initial discovery of the Amarna boundary stelae occurred as early as 1714 when Claude Sicard noted the northwestern stela. Copies of the stelae were made in 1827 and again in the early 20th century, published by Norman de Garis Davies in 1908. Most recently, William Murnane recorded them in detail during field work

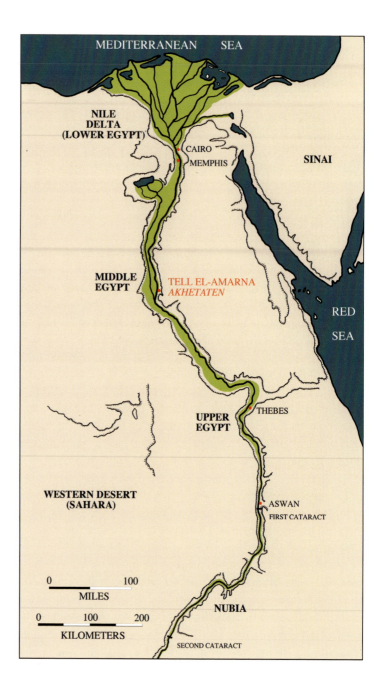

Fig. 36. Map of Egypt showing the location of Tell el-Amarna, ancient Akhetaten.

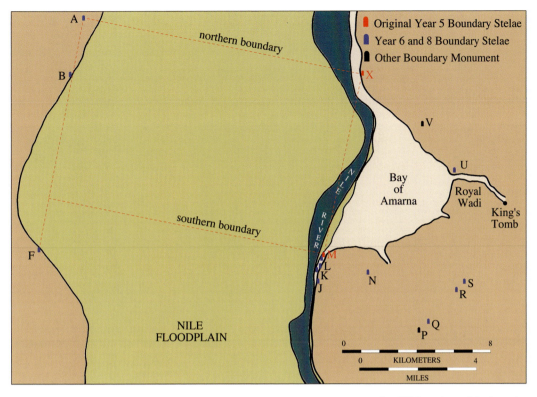

Fig. 37. Locations of the boundary stelae of Amarna, which Akhenaten established in Years 5, 6, and 8 of his reign.

in 1983–85. His publications (1993, 1995) are the primary source of the translations here. The hieroglyphic texts on these stelae include a number of versions of a royal decree, composed largely in the voice of Akhenaten and recording some of the principal events associated with the establishment of the city. By means of these stelae, Akhenaten defined his vision for his new royal capital.

A momentous event occurred in year 5 of Akhenaten's reign: the initial "discovery" of the place Akhenaten would build his capital. The earliest of the boundary markers, two stelae on the eastern side of the Nile and delineating the northern and southern limits of the city, record this event.

> Regnal Year 5, fourth month of the growing season, day 13. . . . On this day, one was in Akhetaten, when his majesty appeared on the great chariot of electrum, just like the Aten when he rises on the horizon and fills the land with his love, he having made a good journey to Akhetaten, his place of the primeval event . . . which he made for himself, his horizon in which his circuit comes into being, where he is beheld with joy while the land rejoices and all hearts exult when they see him.

Fig. 38. Boundary Stela A (dating to Year 6) on the west bank showing the stela flanked by engaged figures of the royal family. Photo courtesy of David. P. Silverman.

This passage is key to understanding why Akhenaten selected this particular place for his future capital. As the Egyptologist Cyril Aldred first observed, the king appears to have chosen this location because the cliffs that frame the bay of Amarna are broken on their eastern side by a prominent *wadi*, or desert valley, today called the Wadi Abu Hasah el-Bahri. Visually, this break in the cliffs forms a striking physical approximation to a classic ancient Egyptian notion, the solar *Akhet* or eastern horizon from which the sun rises every morning. The appearance of this natural land form was apparently Akhenaten's inspiration. Akhenaten identifies the site very literally in the boundary stela as the sun god's "place of the primeval event" (location of solar creation and cyclical rebirth) and "his horizon in which his circuit comes into being" (the point of origin of his daily passage from dawn to dusk). For that reason the name *Akhetaten* (meaning the *Akhet* belonging to Aten) refers primarily to this sacred horizon in the eastern cliffs of Amarna but also came to serve as the name of the city itself. When construction commenced during Year 5, the central city of Amarna was carefully aligned with this solar *Akhet*.

The boundary stelae record that a huge offering ceremony in honor of the Aten immediately followed Akhenaten's chariot ride "to *Akhetaten*": "A great offering was presented to the father, the Aten, consisting of bread, beer, long and short horned cattle, calves, fowl, wine, fruits, incense, all sorts of fresh green plants and everything good in front of the mountain of Akhetaten."

The king's chariot ride and associated offering ceremony to the Aten "in front of the mountain of *Akhetaten*" evidently formed a pivotal event in the mind of the king, as Akhenaten symbolically repeated this moment on the first anniversary of its occurrence and in subsequent years.

What transpired during this momentous event of Akhetaten's discovery in Year 5? Why did the king consider it so important that he periodically repeated the event on its anniversary? Many Egyptologists assume that when Akhenaten arrived at Amarna he simply observed the *akhet* from afar and made his decree for the city's establishment in the area along the desert edge that would later become the century city of Amarna. The text of the Year 5 decree, however, is highly suggestive of a much more direct and spiritual encounter between the king and the Aten. When the texts say that the king arrived in Akhentaten on his great chariot of electrum, "having made a good journey *to the Akhet of Aten*, his place of the primeval event" we may see explicit reference to a royal excursion that took the king out into the sacred *wadi*. It is only logical if the king himself discovered and identified the *wadi* entrance as the horizon of the sun-god that he would have made the trip to venerate the Aten in this magical setting. More than anything else, this mo-

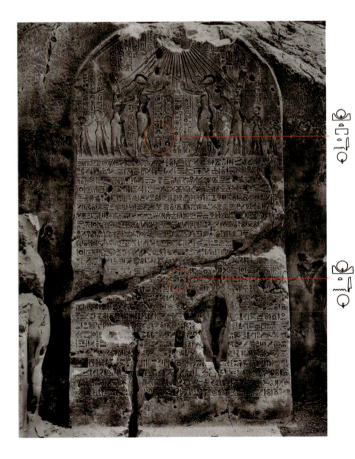

Fig. 39. Boundary Stela S dating to Year 6 shows the designation of the capital city with the hieroglyph Akhet "Horizon." After Davies (1908:pl. 39).

Fig. 40. The royal *wadi* at Amarna, location of the *Akhet* of the Aten. Photo courtesy of David P. Silverman.

ment of communion between king and Aten in the sacred *wadi* may have represented the religious basis for Akhenaten's new capital. It is likely to be this initial journey of Akhenaten to the *wadi* that symbolized the discovery of Akhetaten and an event that the king sought to relive in later years.

The discovery of Akhetaten appears to have been a carefully orchestrated event which linked the establishment of the new city with a symbolic communion between king and Aten in the setting of the sacred eastern horizon of the Aten. The alignment of the city of Amarna with the *wadi* (and the decision to locate the king's tomb within that *wadi*) may ultimately echo this initial moment of near-mystical revelation of the *Akhet* to Akhenaten.

Akhenaten makes it clear that it is the Aten itself who desires a place for his eternal worship and has instructed the king to build the city in this place: "Now it is the Aten, my father who advised me concerning the place of Akhetaten. No official ever advised me concerning it, nor have any people in the entire land advised me concerning it to tell me a plan for making Akhetaten in this distant place. It was the Aten my father who advised me concerning it so that it could be built for him as Akhetaten."

Akhenaten's assembled officials acknowledge that this place is to become the site of a royal city from which Akhenaten and his sole-god will rule Egypt—and, indeed, the entire world. The text states that the Aten divinely sanctions Akhenaten's rulership in "Akhetaten" and that it is in this particular place that the god's commands will emanate through the person of the king:

> May his lordship govern from Akhetaten. May you conduct every land to him. May you tax the towns and islands on

Fig. 41. Akhenaten on his chariot in the Tomb of the Chief of Police of Akhetaten, Mahu, Amarna. The king used his "great chariot of electrum" on which he appeared "like the Aten" in the discovery of the city and later in traveling within his capital. Photo courtesy of Robert K. Ritner.

his behalf. Every city in its entirety belongs to Aten, acting in accordance with what he himself ordains. All lands, all hill countries and the islands of the sea bear tribute, their products on their backs to the maker of their life, when they see the rays which cause one to live. The breath of his love is breathed eternally while his rays are seen and while his lordship does as he pleases and gives commands to you while you are in Akhetaten, rejuvenated like the Aten in the sky forever and ever.

The king then undertook the ritual establishment of the city's boundaries. This activity has fortunately provided us with actual stelae that the king used to demarcate the perimeter of Amarna. He rode to the south and north and ritually marked the locations of the city's boundaries, vowing never to extend the city beyond these limits and never to allow the city to be built in any other location. He also made an oath never to abandon the city for some other place. In so doing he again emphasizes that the site was so significant because the Aten itself had magically revealed the place to him:

Since he casts them [his rays] on me, in life and dominion continually forever, I shall make Akhetaten for the Aten my

Fig. 42. Entrance to the Wadi Abu Hasah el-Bahri, the probable destination of Akhenaten's initial chariot journey and discovery of the *Akhet* in Year 5. Photo courtesy of Robert K. Ritner.

father in this place. I shall not make Akhetaten for him south of it, north of it, west of it or east of it. I shall not go upriver past the southern stela, nor shall I go past the northern stela downstream in order to make Akhetaten. I shall make Akhetaten, for the Aten, my father, on the eastern [side] of the river, the place which he himself made to be enclosed for himself by the mountain, on which he may achieve happiness and on which I shall offer to him. This is it!

Aside from revealing details about the initial discovery of Akhetaten and the establishment of the city's boundaries, the most important feature of the boundary stelae is the description of Akhenaten's vision for what his city would contain, including two main temples for the Aten's worship: "At Akhetaten in this place I shall make the temple named 'House-of-the-Aten' for the Aten my father . . . At Akhetaten in this place I shall make the 'Mansion-of-the-Aten' for the Aten my father. . . . In the Island-of-the-Aten whose jubilees are distinguished at Akhetaten in this place I shall make the 'House-of-Rejoicing' for my father the Aten."

These temples—the "House-of-the-Aten" (Egyptian *Per-Aten*) and the "Mansion-of-the-Aten" (Egyptian *Hut-Aten*)—are the two main religious buildings forming the nucleus of Amarna. Archaeologists call these structures the Great Aten Temple and the Small Aten Temple, respectively. Akhenaten appears to have intended the Small Aten Temple primarily for his personal worship of the Aten. The Great Aten Temple, on the other hand, served in huge public festivals in which many people gathered to witness the worship of the sun god.

Akhenaten also planned special buildings for worship of the Aten. Prominent in his plans were royal "sunshade" temples in honor of prominent royal women. The boundary stelae record that Akhenaten built one of these sunshades for Nefertiti. Scenes and texts in the Tomb of Huya at Amarna record a sunshade belonging to Akhenaten's mother Queen Tiye, and actually depict her first visit to the building. The princesses, including Meritaten (the king's eldest daughter) and Ankhesenpaaten (third daughter and future wife of Tutankhamun), also possessed sunshades.

The king planned the construction of palaces, both for himself and Nefertiti: "At Akhetaten in this place I shall make for myself the residence of the Pharaoh, and I shall make the residence of the king's chief wife."

Finally, in the sacred *wadi* which had evidently drawn Akhenaten to the site, the king planned to build a royal tomb in which the Aten will allow him to celebrate "millions of jubilees," a statement of eternal rulership in the company of the Aten, as it rises daily from its *Akhet* in the east. There too the king intended to place the burials of Nefertiti and his eldest daughter Meritaten: "Let a tomb

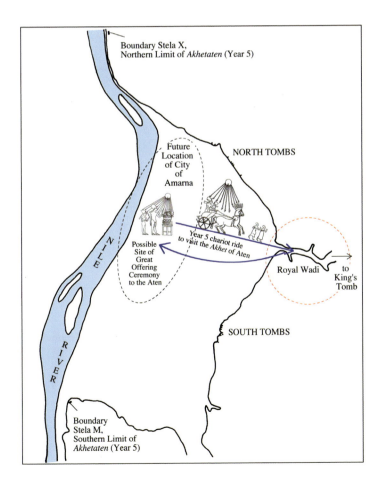

Fig. 43. Diagram showing the possible initial chariot visit of Akhenaten to the *Akhet* of the Aten in Year 5, Day 13, of the fourth month of the growing season.

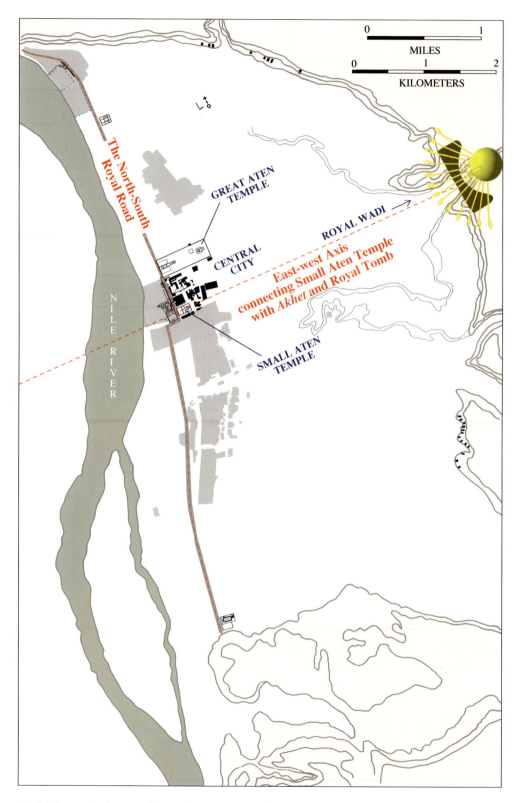

The North-South Royal Road

GREAT ATEN TEMPLE

ROYAL WADI

CENTRAL CITY

East-west Axis connecting Small Aten Temple with *Akhet* and Royal Tomb

NILE RIVER

SMALL ATEN TEMPLE

0   1
MILES

0   1   2
KILOMETERS

Fig. 44. Amarna's alignment showing the intersection in the Central City of the symbolic east-west axis oriented to the royal *wadi* and the north-south axis of the Royal Road.

be made for me in the eastern mountain of Akhetaten, and let my burial be made in it, in the millions of jubilees which the Aten, my father, decreed for me. Let the burial of the king's chief wife Nefertiti be made in it in the millions of years which my father decreed for her. Let also the burial of the king's daughter Meritaten be made in it."

This royal tomb was discovered in 1888, located far into the Wadi Abu Hasah el-Bahri at Amarna. It once contained the burials of Akhenaten, his mother Tiye, and the princess Meketaten (scenes of whose death and mourning decorate part of the tomb's interior: see Figure 2.17). Other royal figures including Nefertiti and Meritaten might also have been buried there since they are the ones Akhenaten specifically mentions in his Year 5 decree in connection with the royal tomb.

In his decree the king also made provisions for burials of other intended occupants of his new city: a sacred bull called the Mnevis, who was associated with the power of the sun god, and for the priests who administered the temples of the Aten: "Let a burial be made for the Mnevis-bull in the eastern mountain of Akhetaten, so that he be buried there. Let there also be made tomb chapels for the greatest of seers and god's father priests of the Aten in the eastern mountain of Akhetaten so that they may be buried in it."

Tombs belonging to priests of the Aten (and many other governmental officials who are not mentioned in the boundary stelae) were, in fact, constructed in the eastern cliffs. These tombs cluster into two main groups, the North Tombs and South Tombs. Decorated with elaborate scenes showing daily activities of the tomb owners, these monuments provide one of the most valuable windows into life in Akhenaten's city. Because the city was abandoned shortly after Akhenaten's death, the tombs never contained their intended burials. The tomb of the sacred Mnevis-bull has never been discovered.

As construction commenced during Year 5 of Akhenaten's reign, the framework of institutional and religious buildings which Akhenaten envisioned would have formed the nucleus of the developing capital. Many of these main buildings were constructed in a core area, the Central City, positioned on a low rise in the desert landscape and may be the "Island-of-the-Aten" that the boundary stelae mention. This central part of Amarna stood in direct alignment with the sacred *Akhet* of the Aten, echoing the quasi-magical event of the site's discovery in Year 5.

So important were the events surrounding the discovery of the city that the king reenacted his initial chariot journey to Akhetaten on its first anniversary in Year 6. At this stage, the city was clearly still in its initial construction. Later boundary stelae describe Akhenaten as residing during that time in a temporary tent built of perishable materials, rather than occupying his permanent palace.

This reenactment of the initial event included a repetition of the king's initial chariot procession to the Akhetaten and offering to the Aten:

> Regnal Year 6, Fourth Month of the growing season, Day 13. . . . On this day one was in Akhetaten in the pavilion of matting that his majesty had made in Akhetaten, the name of which is "Aten-is-Content." His majesty appeared mounted on a great chariot of electrum, like the Aten himself when he rises in the horizon, having filled the two-lands with his love, having made the journey on a good road toward Akhetaten on the first anniversary of its discovery.

Fig. 45. The ascent to the North Tombs at Amarna. Today these private rock-cut tomb chapels are badly damaged but contain elaborate scenes of life in Akhenaten's capital. Photo courtesy of David P. Silverman.

Two years later, in Year 8, Akhenaten again reenacted this ritual of the city's discovery and repeated the demarcation of the city's boundaries. At that time he repaired damage to one of the original stelae and added new inscriptions to the boundary markers. Year 8 may represent the point at which Akhenaten officially occupied his palaces and Amarna where, almost certainly, prince Tutankhaten would be born.

4

AMARNA'S PALACES AND TEMPLES

*I*n this Place I Shall Make the Residence of the Pharaoh

Like royal capitals throughout human history, Amarna was a place of pomp and circumstance. The palaces and temples of Amarna were clearly designed to impress. The city housed the offices of Egypt's central government—the royal treasury, military command, and royal archives. Many of Egypt's wealthiest and most powerful citizens lived in the city.

Through the large scale of the buildings (some structures such as the Great Aten Temple were so big they were never fully completed!) as well as their ornate decoration, the city was intended as a tribute to the life-giving power of the sun god. King Horemheb extensively razed the temples and palaces of Amarna when he took the throne at the end of Dynasty 18, and the growing Nile floodplain and more recently modern local towns and agriculture have irrevocably destroyed large sections of the city's remains. Nevertheless, the ruins of Tell el-Amarna still provide modern archaeologists with more information on the design of a large ancient Egyptian city than anywhere else in Egypt.

Three main structuring principles govern Amarna's overall layout. First is the religious importance attached to the sacred *wadi*, the *Akhet* of the Aten, as recorded in the king's Year 5 boundary stelae. The location of the core of the capital stands in alignment with this *wadi*, forming a symbolic east-west axis that links the center of Amarna with the *wadi* (see Figure 44).

Second, since the city was built on the desert edge, water supply was largely dependent upon wells cut down from the desert surface. In order to reach the water table, it proved unfeasible to construct buildings much more than about half a mile (ca. 1 km) into the desert (the more distant, special-purpose Workmen's Village relied on water carried from the main city). For that reason, the majority of the city straggles in a north-south configuration parallel to the edge of the Nile floodplain.

This orientation was the basis for the city's central artery: an actual north-south avenue. This grand (though not perfectly straight) road, measures approximately 100 to 120 feet (ca. 30-35

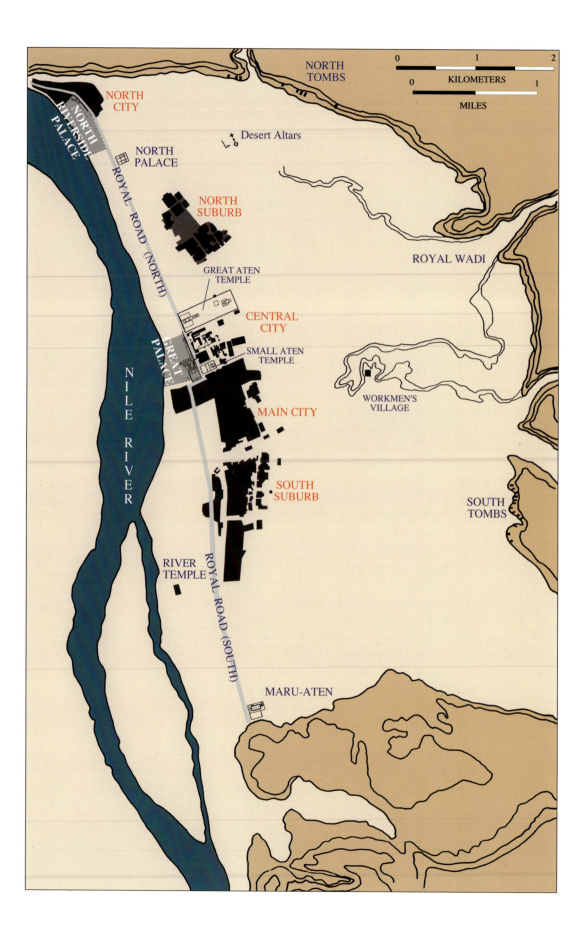

NORTH
TOMBS

0   1   2

KILOMETERS

0   1

MILES

NORTH
CITY

NORTH
RIVERSIDE
PALACE

⊥ ✝ Desert Altars

NORTH
PALACE

NORTH
SUBURB

NILE RIVER

ROYAL ROAD (NORTH)

ROYAL WADI

GREAT ATEN
TEMPLE

CENTRAL
CITY

GREAT
PALACE

SMALL ATEN
TEMPLE

MAIN CITY

WORKMEN'S
VILLAGE

SOUTH
SUBURB

SOUTH
TOMBS

RIVER
TEMPLE

ROYAL ROAD (SOUTH)

MARU-ATEN

m.) wide and ties the different sectors of the city together. It would originally have extended the full distance from the city's northern end to its southern boundary. Essentially all of the known royal buildings at Amarna stood fronting this north-south road, as did the temples dedicated to the Aten. The road therefore formed a Kingsway serving as the main route Akhenaten used in moving between his various palaces and the Aten temples. For that reason, Egyptologists usually call it the Royal Road.

A third important influence on the city's design is the fact that Amarna's low-desert terrain is not uniformly flat. Millennia of water running off of the desert cliffs and flowing across the plain toward the Nile created a series of normally dry but deep and rough gullies. Amarna thus breaks into in a series of sectors with these gullies forming the natural divisions between the different parts of the city. From south to north we therefore designate the South Suburb and Main City (the city's primary residential zones), the

Fig. 46, opposite. Plan of the city of Amarna.

Fig. 47. Plan of Amarna's Central City

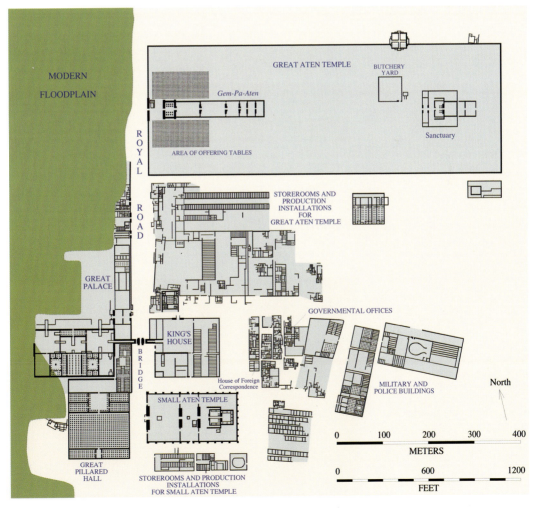

MODERN
FLOODPLAIN

GREAT ATEN TEMPLE

BUTCHERY YARD

Gem-Pa-Aten

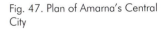

Sanctuary

R
O
Y
A
L

R
O
A
D

AREA OF OFFERING TABLES

STOREROOMS AND PRODUCTION INSTALLATIONS FOR GREAT ATEN TEMPLE

GREAT PALACE

GOVERNMENTAL OFFICES

KING'S HOUSE

B
R
I
D
G
E

House of Foreign Correspondence

MILITARY AND POLICE BUILDINGS

North

SMALL ATEN TEMPLE

0   100   200   300   400

METERS

GREAT PILLARED HALL

STOREROOMS AND PRODUCTION INSTALLATIONS FOR SMALL ATEN TEMPLE

0   600   1200

FEET

Fig. 48. Reconstruction of Amarna's Central City. © David Grandorge.

Central City (containing the temples to the Aten and official buildings), the North Suburb (a residential area), and the North City (a special area containing private residences and royal palaces).

The core of Akhenaten's capital was the area of the Central City. Standing on a low rise in the elevation of the desert, this official quarter of Amarna may be equivalent with the otherwise mysterious term "Island-of-the-Aten" mentioned in the Amarna boundary stelae. The buildings of the Central City are in alignment with the central *wadi* positioned so as to relate symbolically to that important natural feature. Located at the point of convergence between the Royal Road and the east-west axis of the Aten's solar circuit emanating from the *Akhet* of Amarna, the Central City was the place where king and Aten symbolically met and interacted.

Although badly shattered, the ruins of the Central City indicate a core of grand royal and religious buildings, many of which were extensively decorated to express the city's dedication to the Aten. Innumerable stone columns bore the titulary of Akhenaten, Nefertiti, and the Aten in endless repetition. Despite the almost mechanical duplication of stock royal inscriptions, Akhenaten's architects displayed considerable inventiveness. As just one example, the architects created many different types of columns, often using motifs drawn from plant and animal life as well as fabric design. Stone doorways in these royal buildings were rarely plain, but were decorated with texts expressing royal devotion to the sun god.

Two temples dedicated to the Aten dominate the Central City—the Great Aten Temple and the Small Aten Temple, whose construction was already anticipated in Akhenaten's Year 5 decree. The Great Aten Temple is a massive, rectangular walled enclosure, or precinct, 900 feet wide and 2,500 feet long (ca. 270 m by 760 m). It contained a free standing offering structure called the *Gem-Pa-Aten* (the "Aten-Is-Found") flanked by huge fields of offering platforms. To its south and adjacent to a palace-like structure called

Fig. 49. Column fragment from the Central City with the cartouches of Akhenaten, Nefertiti, and the Aten. Most stone elements of Amarna's royal buildings were brightly painted, as was this column, which retains small areas of original red and blue paint. Opponents of these rulers razed their buildings and monuments. Much of our evidence for reconstructing the history of the Amarna Age comes from piecing together small fragments such as this. Sandstone. UPMAA E643. Length 58 cm (22.8 in), height 27 cm (10.6 in), depth 21 cm (8.3 in).

Fig. 50. Column fragment. Inscriptions at the top of the ribbed shaft list the titles of Akhenaten, Nefertiti, and the Aten. UPMAA E865. Amarna, Central City. Limestone. Height 46 cm (18.1 in), width 29 cm (11.4 in), and depth 6 cm (2.4 in).

the King's House lies the Small Aten Temple, the *Hut-Aten* (the "Mansion-of-the-Aten"). Both the Great and Small Aten temples are poorly preserved due to the extensive destruction which the city suffered following the death of Akhenaten. Depictions of these buildings in the decorated rock tombs at Amarna, in combination with excavation of the ruins of the two buildings, reveal a design of entirely unroofed architecture. Although fronted by grand pylons inset with columns and flagpoles in their façades, the interior of both Aten temples consisted of a series of courtyards filled with altars and offering platforms upon which food would be placed. Extensive bakeries and storehouses for producing the god's offerings are located next to the two Aten temples.

Each temple contained a freestanding T-shaped sanctuary at its inner end composed of pillared halls with statues of the royal family. Unlike traditional Egyptian temples, neither contained an actual shrine to house a cult image of the god. The object of worship was not a statue but the visible sun in the sky. The sanctuaries of the Amarna temples thus served primarily as settings for religious rituals emphasizing the divine connections between the Aten and the royal family. These sanctuaries and other stone-built segments of the temples employed the use of *talatat* blocks, small maneuverable limestone blocks. Building by means of talatat had developed early in Akhenaten's reign in his buildings at Thebes. At Amarna this technique greatly increased the speed of constructing the ambitious buildings which the king envisioned (see Figure 3).

One of the most intriguing but badly destroyed royal buildings at Amarna is the Great Palace. Now largely buried and covered by cultivation, the Great Palace appears to have been the primary structure the king used for official state functions and ceremonies. This massive complex ran parallel to the western side of the Royal Road and straddled the locations of the Great and Small Aten

Fig. 51. Column fragments. Many types of columns in the royal buildings display motifs from fabric design, plants, and even animal elements. Amarna. Limestone. From top to bottom: UPMAA E645b. Height 30 cm (11.9 in) and length 9 cm (3.5 in). E849A. Length 48 cm (18.89 in) and width 10 cm (3.9 in). E2211B. Length 28 cm (11 in) and height 16 cm (6.3 in). 2211A. Length 40 cm (15.7 in) and height 10 cm (3.9 in).

Fig. 52. The name and epithets of the Aten decorate two inscribed door lintels from the Central City. Limestone. Top: UPMAA E16181. Height 40 cm (15.7 in) and length 65 cm (25.6 in). Bottom: UPMAA E16180. Height 50 cm (19.7 in) and length 70 cm (26.7 in).

temples. The north-south orientation of the Great Palace is important and occurs also in another Amarna palace, the North Riverside Palace likely served as Akhenaten's actual residence. Both palaces of the pharaoh may have employed this north-south orientation to emphasize the axis of royal authority paralleling the Nile and intersecting with the east-west axis of the Aten. Akhenaten's palaces certainly connected with the Nile. Scenes in Amarna's private tombs show extensive garden areas extending down into the floodplain as well as quays and landing areas for boats attached to the king's palaces.

The Great Palace had a series of open, decorated courtyards that once contained colossal statuary of Akhenaten and Nefertiti. A distinctive feature of the building's architecture is its extensive use of raised platforms and podia. Walled ramps ran up to these

Fig. 53. This block bears the name of king, queen, and the Aten executed in a rapid carving style. UPMAA E16019. Amarna, Central City. Limestone. Height 22 cm (8.7 in), length 52 cm (20.5 in), and width 25 cm (9.8 in).

raised features, with decorated balustrades forming the edges of the ramp. The use of balustrades is a hallmark of Amarna's architecture, also occurring in the Aten temples and other buildings but with particular prominence in the Great Palace. As we see in the Amarna tomb scenes, the front of the balustrade is defined on either side by rounded conical markers. Scenes of the royal family worshipping the Aten decorated the sides of the balustrades. Inscriptions naming the Aten, Akhenaten, and Nefertiti occurred in beautifully sculpted hieroglyphs that ran the length of the upper edges (the railings) of the balustrades. These decorated ramps appear to have been designed as points of royal passage and ascension and indicate the ceremonial functions of the Great Palace.

Fig. 54. Reconstruction of the Great Aten Temple. Photo © David Grandorge.

Fig. 55. Akhenaten and Nefertiti presenting offerings in the forecourt of the Great Aten temple. The pylon of the *Gem-Pa-Aten* with flagpoles and columns stands on the left in front of the royal couple. Photo courtesy of Stephen R. Phillips.

Fig. 56. Reconstruction of the
T-shaped sanctuary of the Great
Aten Temple. Photo © David
Grandorge.

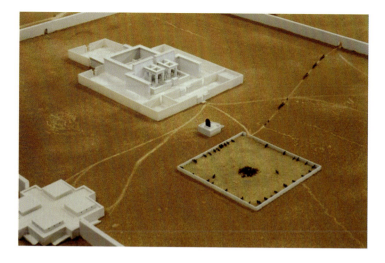

The Penn Museum's collection includes numerous fragments
of these once-magnificent balustrades recovered during Flinders
Petrie's excavations in 1891. In various stones, including red and
black granite, quartzite, and Egyptian alabaster (calcite), the decorated balustrades in the Great Palace employ the early, exaggerated style of Amarna art (characterized by highly elongated heads,
chins, and other parts of the body). The delicately rendered head
of Queen Nefertiti (see Figure 17) exemplifies this striking style in
royal representation. A fragment of a balustrade from the Great
Palace in the Cairo Museum, one of the best-known images of
Amarna artwork, is a more complete example of the theme and
style of these forms. The style of the artwork on the Great Palace
balustrades indicates that building was completed very early: between Years 5 and 8 of Akhenaten's reign.

Many Egyptologists believe the Great Palace served as the main
building in which Akhenaten would have performed his affairs of
state. A bridge spanning the Royal Road connected the palace with
a smaller royal building, the King's House, which sits between the
two Aten temples. The more intimate spaces of this building may
represent a temporary residence which Akhenaten used when he
was present in the Central City. The bridge would have allowed the
king and his attendants to move easily between his private quarters and the ceremonial spaces of the Great Palace.

The Central City also included administrative buildings for
the main departments of the royal government. The best known
of these structures is the House of Royal Correspondence, identified through its stamped bricks showing this name in hieroglyphs.
It was here that a local woman discovered the famous archive of
Akkadian tablets, the "Amarna Letters" in the 19th century. Other
administrative buildings remain more difficult to identify specifi-

cally, although a sector of buildings devoted to the military occur to the east of the main offices of government.

Flanking Amarna's Central City were the primary residential zones: the Main City, South Suburb, and North Suburb. It was in these areas that most of the city's population resided in a mix of grand, walled estates and tracts of smaller houses. Like much of the city, these areas of habitation were never fully completed. The northeastern edge of the North Suburb, for instance, was still growing up to the time the city was abandoned. Parcels of land stood enclosed inside walled compounds, but no houses or buildings had been constructed inside them.

The Central City of Amarna formed the hub of government and the cult of the Aten, but the evidence strongly suggests that Akhenaten did not live in that part of his capital. His actual residential palace appears to have been the now very damaged structure called the North Riverside Palace at the far northern end of

Fig. 57. Fragmentary royal statues may have originally decorated the Aten temples. Amarna, Central City. Top: E2210. Red Granite. Length 9.5 cm (3.7 in) and width 4 cm (1.6 in). Bottom: E2205. Length 10 cm (3.9 in) and width 8 cm (3.1 in).

Fig. 58. Reconstruction of the possible appearance of the Great Palace. Photo © David Grandorge.

the bay of Amarna. Called the North City, this area lies well beyond the North Suburb, 1.5 miles (2.5 km) from the Central City. Archaeologists have traced there the northern end of the Royal Road as it makes its way through a series of administrative buildings. A gateway may once have existed to control land traffic entering the city from the north. The setting of the North City is perhaps the most picturesque area of the Amarna bay, with only a narrow area of land hemmed between the cliffs and the Nile River.

Although almost entirely destroyed, the North Riverside Palace was certainly the building that once dominated the North City's skyline. The structure took the form of a sprawling, walled complex on the western side of the Royal Road. Remains of massive bastioned enclosure walls and a painted gateway suggest that a

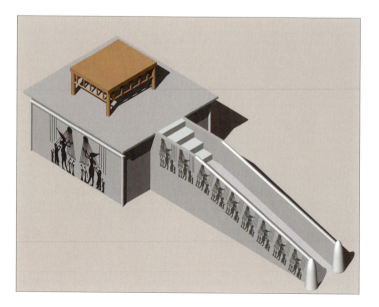

Fig. 59. Three-dimensional reconstruction of the form of the balustraded ramps at Amarna. Reconstruction by Josef Wegner.

royal compound once extended parallel to the Nile. This structure was likely the residential palace of Akhenaten, forming a balancing element to the state palace, the Great Palace, also located on the western side of the Royal Road but in the Central City.

Marking the southern limit of the North City is yet another palace, the North Palace, which is the best preserved of all the royal buildings at Amarna. The North Palace has a symmetrical plan which echoes Egyptian temple design. Inside its entrance (which connects to the Royal Road to the west) once stood a massive pylon, colorfully painted and gilded with details in gold-leaf decoration. Dominating the center of the palace is a large central pool, behind which is a royal residential area containing a throne room on the building's central axis. Some sections of

Fig. 60. Fragment of the tapering, conical end of a balustrade bearing the name of Akhenaten. UPMAA E651. Amarna. Sandstone. Height 11 cm (4.3 in) and width 20 cm (7.9 in).

Fig. 61. Examples of carved balustrades. Top: UPMAA E649. Red granite. Length 9 cm (3.5 in), width 11 cm (4.3 in), and height 9 cm (3.5 in). Bottom: UPMAA E2213. Black Granite. Height 17.2 cm (6.8 in), width 16.4 cm (6.5 in), and depth 10.64 cm (4.2 in).

the building appear to have had administrative and storage functions, but most of the north side of the building shows signs of having been used for maintaining such animals as sheep, goats, gazelles, cattle, and birds. An extensive series of courtyards and chambers contain mangers decorated with images of hoofed animals. Tethering stones also occur in this area of the palace. Such tethering stones often appear in scenes of butchery yards in Amarna's private tombs, though we do not know whether animals housed in the North Palace were tied up for butchery or for other reasons.

The most vibrant of all the scenes of nature discovered at Amarna is a wall mural in the North Palace depicting marsh life and birds. When the Egypt Exploration Society excavated the North Palace between 1923 and 1925, the excavators found this scene decorating

Fig. 62, opposite. Examples of carved Egyptian alabaster balustrades with royal names decorating the upper, rounded surface, and image of worship of the Aten on the side. Calcite. Top left: UPMAA E850. Length 32 cm (12.6 in) and width 13 cm (5.11 in). Top right: E2204a. Length 15.4 cm (6.1 in) and width 13.5 cm (5.3 in). Bottom left: E582. Height 8 cm (3.1 in) and width 6 cm (2.3 in). Bottom right: E1007C. Height 11 cm (4.3 in) and width 7 cm (2.7 in).

Fig. 63. Fragments depicting the royal family worshipping the Aten. Calcite. Top to bottom: UPMAA E471b. Height 11.1 cm (4.4 in) and width 12.1 cm (4.8 in). UPMAA E2204b. Height 14.6 cm (5.6 in) and width 10.5 cm (4.1 in). UPMAA E471a. Height 18.6 cm (7.3 in) and width 12.1 cm (4.8 in). E1007D. Height 12 cm (4.7 in) and width 10 cm (3.9 in).

Fig. 64. Reconstruction of the appearance of residences in Amarna's Main City, view looking north toward the Central City. Photo © David Grandorge.

Fig. 65. A complete scene in the early, exaggerated style occurs on this fragment of a Great Palace balustrade. Cairo Museum TR 30/10/26/12. Crystalline limestone. Height 102 cm (40.2 in), width 51 cm (20.1 in), and depth 15 cm (5.9 in).

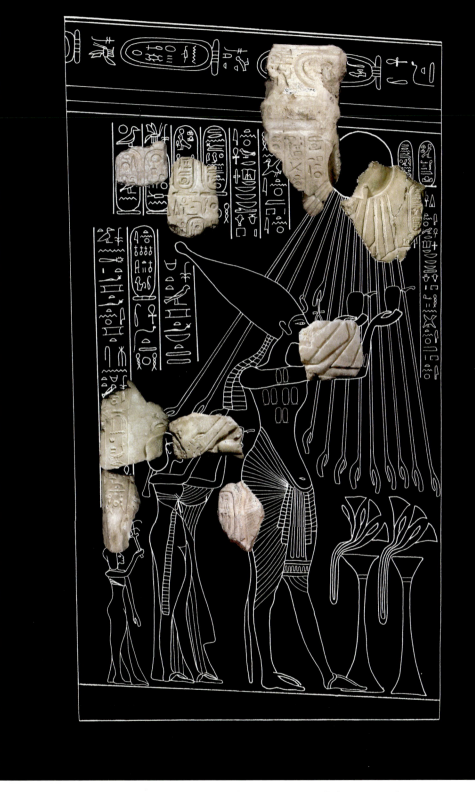

Fig. 66. Reconstruction of the approximate position of alabaster balustrade fragments in the Penn Museum.

Fig. 67. Photograph of the ruins of the North Palace looking north toward the cliffs. Photo courtesy of Robert K. Ritner.

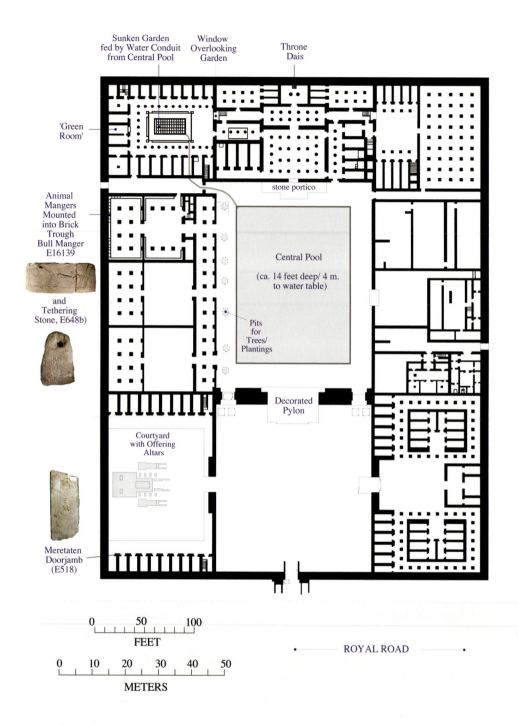

Sunken Garden
fed by Water Conduit
from Central Pool

Window
Overlooking
Garden

Throne
Dais

'Green
Room'

Animal
Mangers
Mounted
into Brick
Trough
Bull Manger
E16139

and
Tethering
Stone, E648b)

Meretaten
Doorjamb
(E518)

stone portico

Central Pool

(ca. 14 feet deep/ 4 m.
to water table)

Pits
for
Trees/
Plantings

Decorated
Pylon

Courtyard
with Offering
Altars

0   50   100
FEET

0   10   20   30   40   50
METERS

ROYAL ROAD

Fig. 68. Plan of the Amarna
North Palace showing the prove-
nience of objects now in the Penn
Museum.

Fig. 69. Decorated relief. The scene shows part of a bull feeding from a manger. Excavators of the North Palace discovered 14 of these objects of different animals feeding. Amarna. Limestone. UPMAA E16139. Height 27 cm (10.6 in), width 73 cm (28.7 in), and depth 13 cm (5.1 in).

a brick chamber, one of a group of 24 rooms positioned around a courtyard containing a sunken garden linked by a water pipe with the building's main pool. The excavators named this decorated chamber the Green Room and suggested it may have been only one part of a large aviary centered on the sunken garden courtyard. A window from the palace's inner residential area overlooked it.

The North Palace appears less likely to have served as any kind of primary royal residence. Rather, it has many elements of a formal ceremonial palace, and, intriguingly, one in which a veritable royal zoo was maintained in a regal setting. It may have been used on a periodic basis for ceremonies and as a pleasure palace. Entering this building through its central pylon, the visitor could have glimpsed the royal occupant enthroned at the innermost end of the palace, behind the building's vast central pool which may have been used in connection with the multitude of animals housed in the building. The entire setting forms a striking combination of royal display alongside a celebration of the human and natural worlds that is seen also so vividly in the Hymn to the Aten: "When day breaks you are risen on the horizon and you shine as the Aten of the daytime. . . . The entire land performs its activities:

all the flocks are content with their fodder, trees and plants grow, birds fly up to their nests, their wings extend in praise for your Ka-spirit." It has even been speculated that one prominent animal occupant of the North Palace could have been the Mnevis-bull, whose presence at Amarna Akhenaten discussed in the original boundary stelae.

By the end of Akhenaten's reign the North Palace appears to have belonged to the king's eldest daughter, Meritaten. Her name occurs on a limestone doorjamb found in the North Palace, carved over and completely obliterating an earlier royal name. This re-carving suggests the North Palace once belonged to a different member of the royal family, possibly Nefertiti herself.

Aside from the royal palaces and temples to the Aten, Amarna included other buildings that blended worship of the sun god with royal activities. Prominent in this category are the royal sunshade temples (so called because the Egyptians named them *Shut-ra*, "shadow-of-the-sun"). We know from the original boundary stelae and scenes in the Tomb of Huya that queens Nefertiti and Tiye were owners of two such buildings. Neither of these has been positively identified in the actual ruins of Amarna.

Fig. 70, opposite. Roughly cut tethering stone inscribed with the name of Akhenaten. UPMAA E648b. Limestone. Height 25.5 cm (10 in) and width 17 cm (5.7 in).

Fig. 71. Scene of a butchery yard with tethering stones next to the sanctuary of the Great Aten temple, from the tomb of Meryre I at Amarna (1903: pl. 11).

butchery
yard
with tethering
stones

Fig. 72. Part of the painted mural decoration of the Green Room showing birds in a marsh land-scape. After watercolor by Davies (1929:pl. 5).

Fig. 73. Ruins of the sunken garden courtyard in the northeast corner of the North Palace with Green Room visible at far side of courtyard. Photo courtesy of Robert K. Ritner.

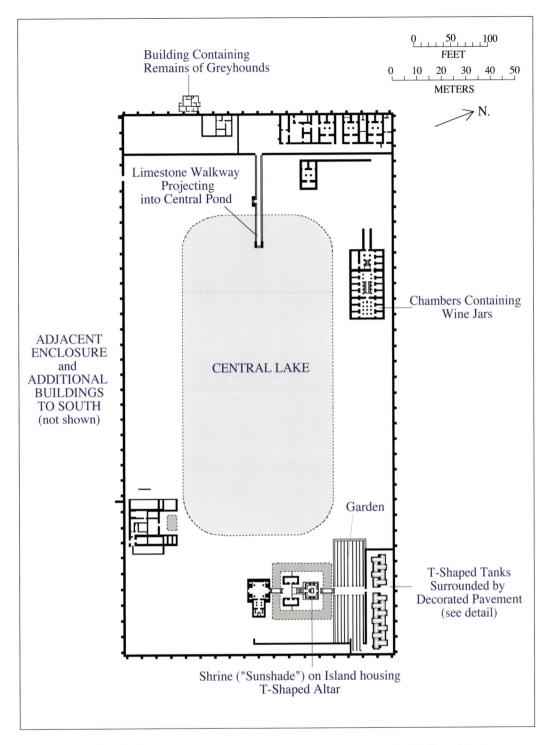

Building Containing
Remains of Greyhounds

0   50   100
FEET

0   10   20   30   40   50
METERS

N.

Limestone Walkway
Projecting
into Central Pond

Chambers Containing
Wine Jars

ADJACENT
ENCLOSURE
and
ADDITIONAL
BUILDINGS
TO SOUTH
(not shown)

CENTRAL LAKE

Garden

T-Shaped Tanks
Surrounded by
Decorated Pavement
(see detail)

Shrine ("Sunshade") on Island housing
T-Shaped Altar

Fig. 74, opposite. Inscribed doorjamb from the North Palace. The hieroglyphic text reads: "the king's daughter Meritaten, may she live." The inscription is cut over an earlier name, possibly that of Queen Nefertiti. UPMAA E518. Limestone. Height 80.5 cm (31.7 in), width 37.4 cm (14.7 in), and depth 27 cm (10.6 in).

Fig. 75. Plan of the *Maruaten* showing some of the main features and location of the decorated pavements adjacent to the sunshade of Princess Meritaten.

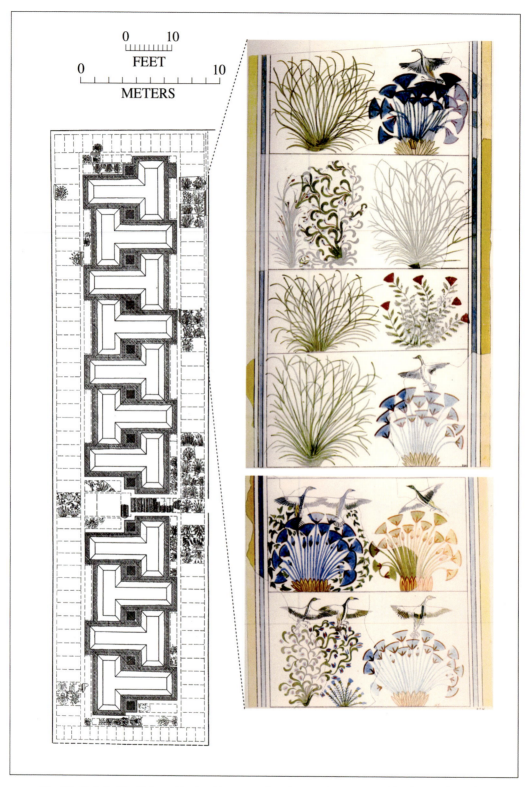

Fig. 76. Detail of the T-shaped tanks with surrounding decorated pavements. After Peet and Woolley (1923:pls. 37, 39).

Other inscriptions record sunshades that belonged to the royal daughters Meritaten and Ankhesenpaaten. Meritaten, the eldest daughter and perhaps favorite of the king, appears to have had two different sunshades, one was connected with the *Per-Aten* and may have stood inside or next to the Great Aten Temple. Her second sunshade forms part of one of the most mysterious royal buildings at Amarna, a structure named *Pa-Maru-en-Pa-Aten*, "The-Viewing-Place-of-the-Aten," which Egyptologists usually refer to simply as the *Maruaten*.

The *Maruaten* is located approximately 2 miles (3.3 km) south of the Central City, at the far southern end of Amarna bay (see Figure 46). The Egypt Exploration Society excavated the *Maruaten* in 1921. Based on its position, the *Maruaten* must have stood on the southern extension of the Royal Road. Although quite remote from the city's core, the *Maruaten* would have formed part of the wider system of temples, palaces, and royal buildings positioned along the city's main north-south thoroughfare.

The overall building consists of two adjacent rectangular brick enclosures. The main enclosure contains a massive artificial lake with remains of a stone causeway that projected out over the wa-

Fig. 77. Painted floor panel from the *Maruaten*. UPMAA E15722. Amarna. Plaster, paint. Width 85 cm (33.5 in).

ter. Extensive areas of planted trees and gardens surround the lake on all sides, suggesting that the *Maruaten* formed a lush scene of greenery in the desert landscape. An intriguing small building next to the main enclosure of the *Maruaten* contained the skeletal remains of dozens of greyhounds (leading the original excavators to suggest the royal kennels were part of the Maruaten). Rooms in one of the buildings inside the main enclosure contained hundreds of wine jars with ink labels naming various institutions at Amarna that had supplied the wine.

The best-preserved elements of the *Maruaten* are located in the northeast corner of the main enclosure where a small artificial island was created with a surrounding moat. On this island stood a columned, stone cult building or kiosk. Adjacent were plots for a formal planted garden and a courtyard containing 11 T-shaped interlocking plastered tanks. The pavement surrounding these tanks bore painted decorations of water plants and wild birds. This type of plastered floor decoration occurred in many of the royal buildings at Amarna and, again, can be seen as a visual expression of the ideas put forth in the Hymn to the Aten which dwells on the dependence of all earthly life on the radiance of the Aten. The name *Maruaten* emphasizes that the building formed a

Fig. 78. Painted floor panel from the *Maruaten*. UPMAA E15726. Amarna. Plaster, paint. Height 103 cm (40.6 in), width 120 cm (47.2 in), depth 7 cm (2.8 in).

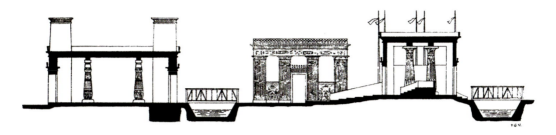

Fig. 79. Reconstruction by the original excavators of the sunshade building in the *Maruaten*. After Peet and Woolley (1923: pl. 30).

setting for royal veneration of the sun god. It is possible that the 11 T-shaped tanks in combination with the kiosk (together forming a group of 12) represent the life-giving energy of the Aten through all 12 months of the calendar year.

Fragments of the stone kiosk bear inscriptions naming the *Shut-ra* of Princess Meritaten, leading us to believe that this building represents her sunshade. The building had a series of decorated screen walls set between columns and a cornice decorated with rows of inlaid cobras.

One of the most important Amarna Period objects in the Penn Museum's collection is associated with the sunshades of the women of Amarna. Since 1891 the Museum has housed a large quartzite slab, usually identified as a stela, with its provenience previously not clear.

The object bears images of Akhenaten and Meritaten. Queen Nefertiti does not appear at all. The royal figures and disk of the Aten are deeply cut in silhouette style which originally contained colored inlays of faience and possibly semiprecious materials. The scenes, unfortunately badly eroded and partially hacked out, show Akhenaten offering to the Aten. Meritaten, shaking a sistrum, follows behind her father. Most of the inscriptions are identifying labels providing the names of the Aten, the king, and the princess. At the top of the scene, however, is a revealing inscription which states: "Aten, distinguished in festivals, lord of all that which the Aten encircles, lord of heaven, lord of earth, in the Sunshade of the king's daughter of his body, his beloved, Meritaten, in [word unclear, ancient text is broken in this spot] Akhetaten."

This inscription identifies this object as originally belonging to one of the sunshades of princess Meritaten at Amarna. Now appearing as a round-topped stela, the piece was originally a rectangular slab and formed the doorway into a decorated shrine or kiosk. Remains of the carved base of a cornice suggest this object was the doorway into an unroofed kiosk building akin to the structure in the *Maruaten*. The same deep-

Fig. 80. Painted row of cobras. Many royal buildings at Amarna were decorated with such rows depicting the royal cobra (*uraeus*). UPMAA E14943. Amarna, Central City. Limestone and pigment. Height 12.7 cm (5 in), width 11.7 cm (4.6 in), and depth 6.7 cm (2.6 in).

sunk silhouette style of the figures also occurs on fragments of Meritaten's sunshade in the *Maruaten*. It is highly probable that the Penn Museum's fragment is in fact part of Meritaten's other, hitherto undiscovered, sunshade at Amarna.

When Amarna was abandoned during the reign of Tutankhamun its great royal buildings were neglected and began to decay. In the reign of King Horemheb at the very end of Dynasty 18, the political reaction against Akhenaten culminated with extensive razing of the temples and palaces of Amarna. Stonework—the decorated *talatat* blocks and other masonry like the quartzite slab from Meritaten's sunshade—was carted off, particularly to the nearby city of Hermopolis, just 10 miles (17 km) north of Amarna, where archaeologists discovered much of it. What remained on the site was badly smashed, a mere shadow of the once-grand city of the Aten.

Fig. 81. Line drawing of the quartzite Amarna stela in the Penn Museum. UPMAA E16230.

5

AMARNA—A CITY OF PAGEANTRY

*B*ehold, *They Have Become People of Gold*

In traditional Egyptian religion the year was full of festivals. During these events, which occurred on special days of the calendar such as the New Year, the gods emerged from their temples, carried out in public display and celebration. These were planned moments when Egypt's people could witness and interact with the divine beings that affected their lives and destiny. When Akhenaten replaced Egypt's long-established religious framework with the sole worship of the Aten, this fundamental public aspect of Egyptian life suddenly vanished. What did Akhenaten offer the people of Egypt in place of their hallowed festivals?

In a religion where all life on earth depended on the radiance emanating from the Aten, and in which the direct worship of the sun god was the exclusive preserve of Akhenaten, the king and royal family now occupied the role of Egypt's traditional gods. Akhenaten appears to have offered himself, his wife, and daughters as the objects of devotion and worship for the common people. Stelae and statues of the royal family stood in shrines and pavilions in private houses at Amarna, indicating that the royal family were venerated in a way similar to that of divinities.

Further extension of this idea appears to have been royal displays in which Akhenaten, Nefertiti, and their daughters appeared in carefully orchestrated events where their subjects could see them. Witnessing the king's movements in the capital was apparently meant to replace Egypt's traditional gods' festivals.

The layout of Amarna played an important role in bringing about this change. The king's architects designed the city with interest in balance and order. The boundary stelae show considerable concern for the city's overall dimensions and symmetry:

> Now as for Akhetaten, starting from the southern stela as far as the northern stela, measured between stela to stela on the eastern side of Akhetaten, it amounts to six *iteru* [a measure of distance], and one and three quarter rods and four cubits. Starting from the southwestern stela of Akhetaten to

Fig. 82. Scene from the Temple of Amun. The god Amun-Re in his barque during the Opet Festival, one of the grandest of Egypt's many traditional festivals prior to and after the Amarna Period. Luxor, Thebes. Photo courtesy of David P. Silverman.

the northwestern stela upon the western side of Akhetaten it amounts to six *iteru*, one and three quarter rods, and four cubits, the same exactly.

Akhenaten's architects recreated the distances that had long defined the ritual setting of Thebes. They replicated the distances between the state temples of Amun-Re at Thebes (Luxor Temple and Karnak Temple), integrating them into Amarna'a design. Why would they do this?

In the traditional festivals of Thebes, distances between these temples represented the route traveled by the god in his periodic festival processions. By recreating these same distances at Amarna, Akhenaten was forming a place where his own daily routes and movements might become a substitute for the processions of the now-abandoned gods. Amarna was a setting for the daily "festival" appearance of the pharaoh and "his father," the Aten itself, superseding the old festivals of Amun-Re.

Decorations on Amarna's rock chapels reveal that one of the most important events of public display of the royal family was a chariot procession, which ideally happened every day. The scenes of this event typically show the king and queen traveling from the palace in chariots to worship the Aten in the Central City, then returning to the royal residence. Behind Akhenaten and Nefertiti follow royal family members and a vast royal entourage. Although

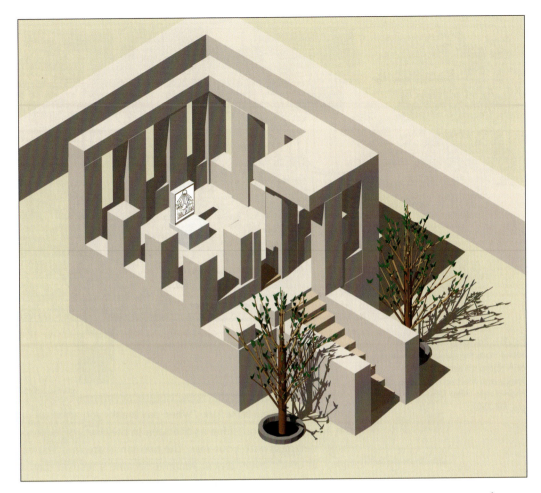

Fig. 83. Reconstruction of a private garden shrine in an Amarna elite estate. Shrines took many forms, but most served in veneration of the royal family.

he never appears explicitly in these scenes, this central activity of royal life at Amarna is one that young Prince Tutankhaten also would have participated in. The chariot procession took the king down the main north-south Royal Road. Surrounded by military and police escorts, this royal progression was obviously not a moment of intimate interaction between Akhenaten and his subjects but was meant to put the royal family on view for adulation by their subjects. Spectators stand on the fringes, bowing and genuflecting as the royal family passes by.

The ancient descriptions of this event make a clear equation between the king and the Aten: "His majesty appears on the great chariot of electrum, just like the Aten when he rises on the horizon and fills the land with his love." Instead of a calendar filled with gods' processions, the people of Amarna saw the king and royal family appear every day along with the rising of the Aten in this newly minted divine cycle. Like many of Akhenaten's practices, the

lier in the 20th century, scholars believed that the main example
sat within the bridge that crosses between the Great Palace and
the King's House in Central City. The wide span of the Royal
Road would provide a spacious, open public area for events
such as the conferral of the "gold of reward." Egyptologists now
doubt the accuracy of this otherwise attractive reconstruction.
The King's House, though highly damaged, is another possible
location, in that a more secluded garden setting may have served
to show the royal family before a more select group.

As a royal capital Amarna would have regularly hosted special
events of great pageantry. While we shall never know the majority
of these grand ceremonies, two of the decorated rock chapels at
Amarna (the tomb chapels of Meryre II and Huya) contain scenes
and inscriptions that record what is undoubtedly the single most
impressive event of royal pageantry known to have occurred at

Fig. 86. Detail of depiction of
the palace with the Window of
Appearances in the Tomb of
Panehesy at Amarna. After Davies
(1904:pl. X).

Fig. 87. Amarna tomb scene showing the Window of Appearances with banners blowing in the breeze. Photo courtesy of Stephen R. Phillips.

Amarna: a great parade of foreign tribute. The texts inform us that this occurred in Year 12, Month 6, Day 8 of Akhenaten's reign.

The scenes show Akhenaten and Nefertiti being carried to the event, their thrones placed on special carrying chairs decorated with sphinxes, hoisted aloft on poles by rows of bearers. Receiving tribute, the royal family appears on a covered dais. Akhenaten and Nefertiti sit side by side with their six daughters standing behind them. Also still alive at Amarna, and present during this event, was Akhenaten's mother, Queen Tiye. The carrying chairs of the royal family are parked beside the royal dais and guarded by royal attendants. The scenes show large numbers of foreigners—Syrians, Hittites, and Aegean peoples (Mycenaean Greeks and Minoans)—who deliver tribute from the northern lands, Libyans from the west, and Nubians and Puntites (men from the land of Punt on the Red Sea) who bring tribute from the south. Piles of offering goods—including precious vessels, chariots, horses, cattle, animal skins, gold, and weaponry—sit before the king. Images of men dancing and

Fig. 88. An earlier reconstruction of the bridge between the Great Palace and King's House with the Window of Appearances and gold of reward ceremony. After Pendlebury (1938:pl. 12).

some fighting with one another provide a hint of the color and clamor that would have occurred as part of this ceremony.

Egyptologists have long debated what this special Year 12 parade of foreign tribute signifies and where at Amarna it might have occurred. The ceremony may have taken place inside the Great Palace, or, given the obviously large crowds involved, in a specially prepared parade ground. One area near the North City called the Desert Altars offers a possible location for staging this event (see Figure 46). Evidence suggests that such grand tribute ceremonies (which also happened in earlier reigns of the 18th Dynasty) generally occurred in connection with crowning the pharaoh. One theory (based on a long coregency between Akhenaten and his father) proposes that Year 12 was when Amenhotep III actually died. In this case, the foreign tribute ceremony may have been part of the ceremonies reaffirming Akhenaten's crowning as sole ruler of Egypt. Most scholars now discount this possibility due to a lack of confirming evidence.

Other scholars favor the idea that Nefertiti (who mysteriously disappears after Year 12) was elevated in rank to that of coregent with her husband around this time. Perhaps the Year 12 tribute ceremony could represent some of the events that celebrated this change in her status and recognized her as pharaoh alongside Akhenaten (indeed, in these scenes she is seated in parallel with Akhenaten, though largely obscured behind the figure of her husband).

Despite the wealth of information available to us regarding what happened, the nature of the evidence is such that we cannot conclusively determine why the Year 12 ceremony occurred and what the event signified. It was clearly a major celebration of kingly power and an event of pomp and pageantry that the people of Amarna witnessed alongside many others who had journeyed for months in advance from foreign lands far beyond Egypt's borders. Akhenaten may perhaps have seen the Year 12 ceremony as a literal fulfillment of his grand design when he declared on the boundary stelae that the entire world belonged to the Aten: "all lands, all hill countries, and the islands in the midst of the sea bear tribute, their products on their backs to the maker of their life, when they see the rays which cause them to live."

Whatever the Year 12 tribute ceremony meant, it represented something of a turning point in the fortunes of Akhenaten's holy experiment. Not only did Nefertiti disappear shortly after this event, but another of Akhenaten's wives, Queen Kiya, also vanished. Akhenaten's second daughter, Princess Meketaten, died around this time and was buried in the royal tomb in the great *wadi*. Some speculate that Akhenaten's family may have been killed by the plague which was ravaging Syria and the Near East at this time (perhaps even brought to Amarna by rats that came with the large numbers of foreign visitors).

This was not a time of complete misfortune for the royal family, since Prince Tutankhaten was born around this time. Some

Fig. 89. Partially reconstructed scene of Akhenaten and Nefertiti seated on carrying chairs on their way to Year 12 tribute ceremony, Tomb of the Overseer of the Royal Harem and of the Two Treasuries, and the Steward of the Great Royal Wife, Tiye, Huya, at Amarna. After Davies (1903-1908:pls. xii-iv, vii).

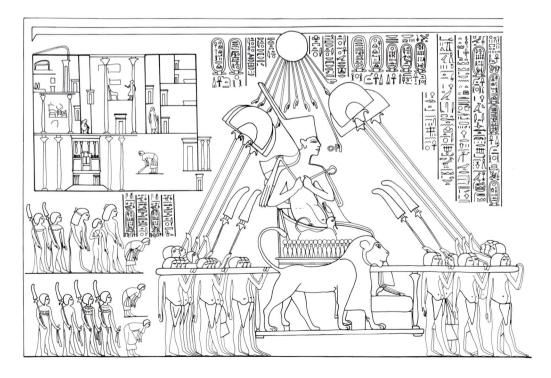

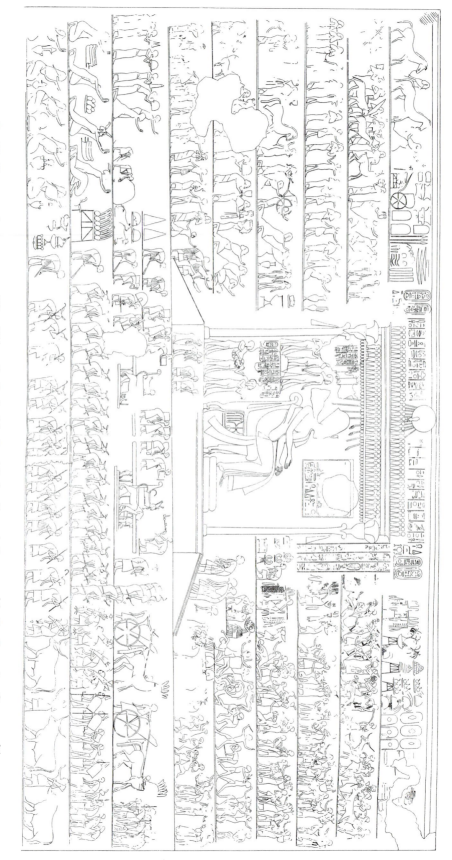

Fig. 90. The great tribute ceremony of Year 12 from the Tomb of the Royal Scribe, Steward, Overseer of the Two Treasuries, Overseer of the Royal Harem of the Great Royal Wife, Nefertiti, Meyre II, at Amarna. After Davies (1903-1908:pls. xxxvii-xl).

Fig. 91. Amarna relief fragment. The original scene of which only a small part survives depicted rows of worshippers or attendants at an event that probably included Akhenaten and Nefertiti. UPMAA E854. Amarna, Central City. Sandstone. Height 15 cm (5.9 in), width 14 cm (5.5 in), and depth 6.5 cm (2.6 in).

have even speculated that images of a baby held by a nurse in the scenes of the death of Princess Meketaten might be the young Tutankhaten (see Figure 35). Tutankhaten's early childhood would undoubtedly have included the spectacle of Amarna and his father's devotion to the worship of the Aten.

Only five years later, Akhenaten himself died. His city of palaces and pageantry was abandoned shortly thereafter as Egypt sought refuge in its traditional gods and the reinstatement of their long-enduring festivals. This was a full reversal that would culminate two years after Akhenaten's death when Tutankhaten took the throne, altered his name to Tutankhamun, and reestablished Egypt's religious center at Thebes.

6

A Place of Artisans and Administrators— Daily Life at Amarna

A *s for What is Inside this City, It Belongs to My Father and I Shall Not Go Past It*

When tourists visit Amarna today, the site appears to be a vast, empty desert plain. Little now remains on the surface to indicate that 3,300 years ago it was a bustling and vital city with a population of 20,000 to 50,000. Amarna was not a typical ancient Egyptian urban center. Built quickly, its population came from other cities throughout Egypt at the command of their king, Akhenaten. Inhabited for roughly a 20 year period, its residents abandoned the site shortly after the end of the reign of Akhenaten and returned to their original homes elsewhere in Egypt.

During its brief life span Amarna, like all major cities, was a busy place filled with noise, activity, manufacturing, and farming. It contained not only temples and palaces, but also large suburbs where the non-royal component of the population lived. Residents of the city consisted of important government officials and administrators, as well as artisans, laborers, servants, fishermen, and farmers. Since later Egyptians did not reoccupy the city, preservation at Amarna is very good. Studies of its archaeological remains provide an intriguing picture of life in an ancient Egyptian settlement, albeit an atypical one. Additional information about the daily life of the city's inhabitants appears in the detailed scenes of the city that decorate the rock-cut tombs.

The majority of the population at Amarna lived in two main housing areas located to the north and south of the Central City (see Figures 46 and 47). Known as the North Suburb and the Main City (or South Suburb), these neighborhoods grew in an organic way. While planned grids with main streets characterize royal areas of the city, non-royal living areas are more complex. Large houses abut smaller dwellings, a pattern that indicates an economically diverse population living side by side. Despite the organized nature of the Central City, it is interesting to note that many of the king's important officials did not live in close by the palace. Prominent officials such as the vizier Nakht and the High Priest Panehesy resided in houses far from the palace. These men must have commuted to their places of employment, and tomb

Fig. 92. View of the modern site of Amarna taken from the cliffs that ring the desert plain. Photo courtesy of Robert K. Ritner.

scenes record the city's inhabitants making daily chariot rides. Archaeologists have also located the houses of other important bureaucrats. The residence of the military officer, Ranefer, the chief charioteer, was relatively small, while that of the commander of troops, Ramose, was nearby and slightly larger. The home of the Overseer of the Builders, Maanatuef, was in the Main City and was modest, while that of the Overseer of Works, Hatiay, which was in the North Suburb was not completed.

Regardless of the wealth of their owners and the size of the houses, most Amarna residences consisted of mud brick with some stone elements. The homes featured a central square living room, usually with a low brick dais or bench built along one wall. One or more wooden columns on a stone column base supported the ceilings. Around this central room were other living spaces, including outer reception rooms, storage chambers, and private living quarters and bedrooms. Recent research indicates that many of the houses likely had 2 or more stories. With few exceptions, gypsum plaster whitewash covered the walls, and, if there were painted decorations, the motifs seemed limited to geometric patterns. Ideally, these houses stood within a private walled courtyard where homeowners and their servants carried out additional domestic operations. The courtyards could contain granaries, pens for animals, kitchens, a well, and a garden, in addition to additional storage and work areas. Some of the wealthier homes included accommodations for extended family members or household staff. The large home of the vizier Nakht at Amarna was a mansion-style residence typical of the type of dwelling the upper class owned. Measuring 85 feet square (26 m square), the house consisted of 30 rooms on the ground floor alone. A second level would have increased this size significantly. A garden, a pool, and a private chapel to the Aten fronted the house.

Perhaps the best-known non-royal resident of the city of Amarna was a man named Tuthmosis, among whose titles were the King's Favorite, Master of Works, and Sculptor. Apparently the court-appointed sculptor for Akhenaten, Tuthmosis and his studio of artisans created royal sculpture on commission from the king. His fame comes from a discovery that a German archaeological expedition made in 1912 when it uncovered the remains of an im-

Fig. 93. Reconstruction of the North Suburb of Amarna, after illustration in Frankfort and Pendlebury (1933:pl. XVII).

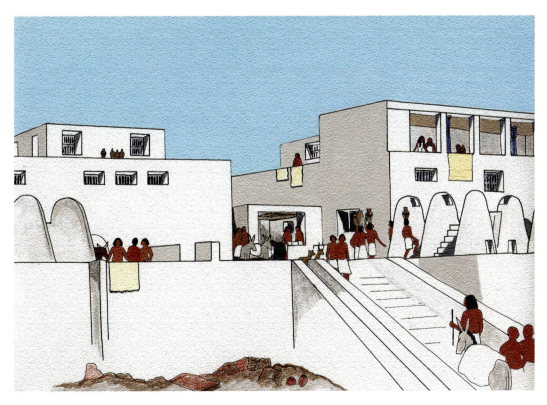

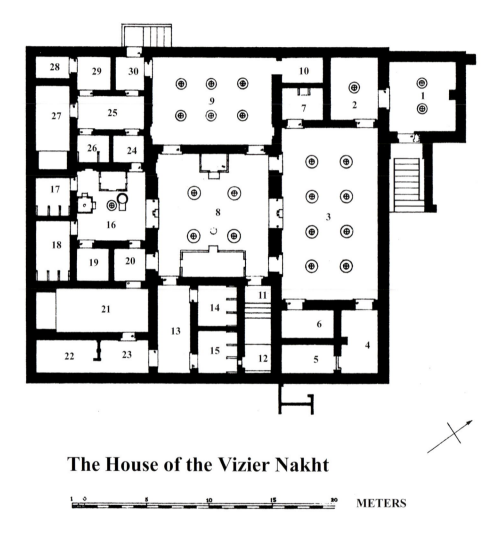

The House of the Vizier Nakht

METERS

Fig. 94. Ground plan of house
(K.50.1) of the vizier, Nakht. After
Peet and Woolley (1923:pl. III).

Fig. 95. Painted reconstruction by F. G. Newton of the interior of Nakht's house. After Peet and Woolley (1923:pl. IV).

pressive mansion-style house and studio located near the more modest homes and workshops of other artisans. An artifact found in a pit in the courtyard of the house bearing the name "Tuthmosis" served to identify this house with the sculptor.

During the excavation, the archaeologist Ludwig Borchardt came upon a storage room with over 50 works of art including the famous painted limestone bust of Nefertiti now in the Egyptian Museum in Berlin (see Figure 17). When inhabitants abandoned the city Tuthmosis did the same, leaving with his most valuable tools. But he left behind images of the disgraced royal family

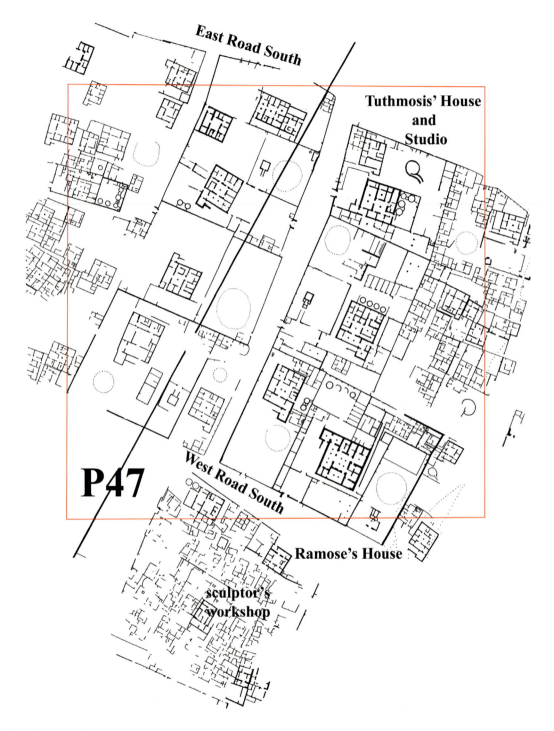

East Road South

Tuthmosis' House
and
Studio

P47

West Road South

Ramose's House

sculptor's
workshop

Fig. 96. Ground plan locating
the House and Studio of the
Sculptor Tuthmosis. Other nearby
workshops and large estate-style
houses can be seen in the area
designated P. 47. After Kemp and
Garfi (1993: map no. 7).

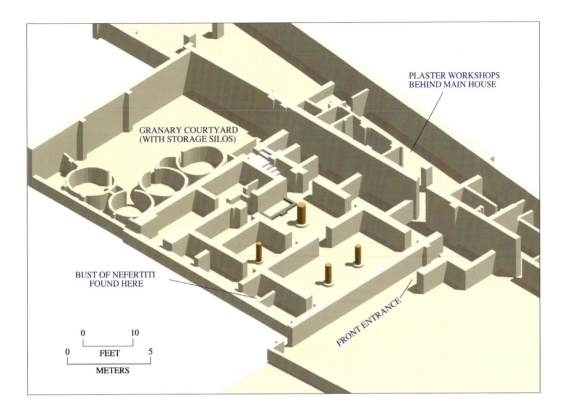

PLASTER WORKSHOPS
BEHIND MAIN HOUSE

GRANARY COURTYARD
(WITH STORAGE SILOS)

BUST OF NEFERTITI
FOUND HERE

FRONT ENTRANCE

0   10
FEET   5
METERS

Fig. 97. Reconstruction of House
of the Sculptor Tuthmosis.

(Akhenaten, Nefertiti, and the princesses), Akhenaten's successor,
Smenkhkare, as well as portraits of other inhabitants of the city.
The sculptor had evidently deposited this material that he no longer needed in a small storeroom before he departed his workshop
forever.

Comprised of three materials—quartzite, limestone, or gypsum plaster—27 of the 50 artworks were of gypsum plaster; 23
of the pieces were heads or faces, seven of which are royal male
heads and two are images identified as Nefertiti. Ten images depict non-royal males. Archaeologists also found three almost life-
size quartzite heads of princesses in Tuthmosis's studio.

Based on these finished or nearly finished works of art and
from debris in the workshop area, it seems that Tuthmosis received
commissions to make particular types of statuary. This studio produced stone heads and limbs for the production of composite statues. In these works, different body parts would have appropriately
colored stones for each of the elements, which would fit together to
form a complete statue. The studio also cast clay models in plaster in advance of a stone sculpture. Artisans made these casts for
the king's or chief sculptor's final approval before completing the
artwork. Flinders Petrie found a similar gypsum head of Akhenaten

Fig. 98, Amarna royal figure. The areas around the eyes and eyebrows of this sculpted head of an Amarna Royal Family member once contained inlays. Penn Museum's 1915 Coxe expedition excavated the site of Mit Rahineh. Cairo Museum JE 45547. Photo courtesy of David P. Silverman. Quartzite. Height 18 cm (7.1 in), width 15.5 cm (6.1 in), depth 21 cm (8.3 in).

during his excavations at the site that he termed a "death mask." In all likelihood, this "death mask" represents another example of a cast produced during the sculptural process. Even the famous bust of Nefertiti seems to be a sculptor's trial work rather than a finished object. While the piece is beautifully painted and intact, except for some losses around the ears, the left eye lacks its inlay. Studies suggest that this bust never had an inlaid eye and that this work of art—the definitive image of the queen—served primarily as a sculptor's model (see Figure 17).

Tuthmosis's estate and workshop are not the only evidence for the existence of sculptors at Amarna. Excavations located another sculpture workshop at the Ipu estate where archaeologists found pieces of statuary and tools, including copper chisels and stone drill heads and other materials such as inlays and unfinished

Fig. 99. Cast of Head of Akhenaten. Flinders Petrie found the original at Amarna. Artists made these casts of clay trial sculptures in order to correct them before completing the final artwork. UPMAA E647. Plaster. Height 15 cm (5.9 in), width 16 cm (6.3 in), and depth 2.5 cm (1 in).

Fig. 100. Line drawing of the
scene of the sculptors at work in
the Tomb of Huya. After Davies
(1906:pl. XVIII).

stone vessels. An object in the yard, inscribed with the name "Ipu," helped to identify this structure as part of the Ipu estate.

Amarna's tomb decorations also provide information about the sculptor's workshops. For example, scenes from Huya's Tomb show Iuty, a sculptor, working with other artists. Sitting on a low stool, Iuty paints a statue of Princess Baketaten, the daughter of Queen Tiye. This statue in the scene is remarkably similar to another sculpture of an Amarna princess in the Penn Museum's collection (see Figure 124). Iuty has the title "Overseer of Sculptors" while the label "Sculptor" identifies the subordinate figures. Another sculptor carves a head for a composite statue, while others work on stone vases and furniture legs. The scenes contain a variety of tools such as brushes, palettes, chisels and adzes, mortars, polishing stones, drill heads, scrapers, paint bowls, stamps, and knives. All of these images correspond to actual implements found in Amarna workshops.

Fig. 101. Pear-shaped vessel. Egyptians in the New Kingdom often used cream-colored translucent Egyptian alabaster for their vessels. This type of container with a flat rim first appeared early in the 18th Dynasty and remained popular until the end of the New Kingdom, around 1075 BCE. UPMAA E652. Amarna. Calcite. Height 9.45 cm (3.7 in) and diameter 7.39 cm (2.9 in).

Fig. 102. Unfinished statue.   This work in progress depicts a servant carrying a heavy burden on his head. UPMAA 29-209-2. Amarna. Limestone. Height 21.5 cm (8.5 cm), width 10.5 cm (4.1 in), and depth 10.2 cm (4 in).

Fig. 103. Found in House P46.9, this palette served as a grinding stone for minerals the Egyptians used for cosmetic eye paint. Painters and scribes also used palettes to grind their pigments. UPMAA 2003-34-420. Amarna. Slate. Height 13 cm (5.1 in), width 7.7 cm (3 in), and depth 1.2 cm (.5 in).

Other areas of the city produced pottery, and evidence suggests that faience production and glassmaking were also key industries that would have helped support the economy of the new city.

Already in the reign of Amenhotep III the words "dazzling" and "gleaming" (Egyptian *tjehen*) described the Aten. The Egyptians used a related word to refer to faience (*tjehenet*), a composite glazed material that embodied the shiny, sparkling qualities that Akhenaten associated with his sun god. Not surprisingly, the city of Amarna became a major center of faience and glass production. A large number of artisans also dealt with the huge volumes of decorative elements such as inlays used in the royal buildings, statuary, and stelae. Excavations uncovered large numbers of faience molds, particularly in the North Suburb region of Amarna, attesting to the massive output of small objects in faience. Artisans likely used many of these locally, but trade throughout Egypt and abroad accounted for the dispersal of others. By the Amarna Period, faience making had existed for millennia in Egypt; however, glass working was a new technology during the 18th Dynasty, when Egyptian artisans began to produce beautifully modeled, multicolored glass vessels. They used a technique in which they

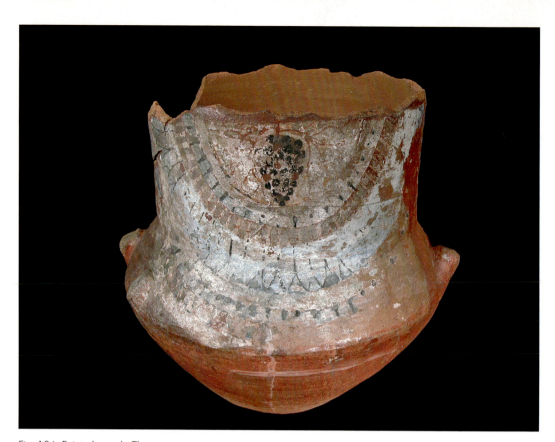

Fig. 104. Painted vessel. The decoration on the jar depicts grapes, a fruit that may have symbolized fertility. Pottery with painted decoration of floral designs came into vogue in the late 18th Dynasty. UPMAA E17888. Amarna. Ceramic, paint. Height 29.2 cm (11.5 in) and diameter 27 cm (10.6 in).

Fig. 105. Ring bezel. The top of this ring takes the form of the *prenomen* of Tutankhamun (throne name: Nebkheprure) in a cartouche. Its bright blue color may have symbolized resurrection. UPMAA E811. Amarna. Blue faience. Height 2 cm (.8 in), width 1.2 cm (.5 in), and depth .5 cm (.2 in).

Fig. 106. Detail of the head of Akhenaten. This fragment from a monumental relief depicts the king and his daughter, Meritaten, worshipping the Aten. UPMAA E16320. Amarna. Quartzite. Height 231.9 cm (91.3 in), width 66 cm (26 in), and depth 24 cm (9.4 in).

Fig. 109. Wooden mallet. Found in the front hall of House 8 in the Workmen's Village, this tool would have been used by artisans and craftsmen in activities requiring pounding. UPMAA 2003-34-384. Amarna. Height 26.5 cm (10.4 in), width 13.7 cm (5.4 in), and depth 13 cm (5.1 in).

cutting and decorating of the royal tomb located far into the royal *wadi* as well as the private tombs in the north and south groups. It is interesting to note that unlike other parts of Amarna, people still lived in this village through the reign of Tutankhamun. Scholars have alternatively suggested that the people of this village may have served as police monitoring the boundaries of the city during its active life span. This village has also provided insight into daily life at Amarna through the well-preserved finds of its small households.

Despite all of Akhenaten's efforts in founding this magnificent new capital, its citizens largely abandoned the city during the early years of the reign of Tutankhamun, taking most of their essentials and valuables with them. Over time, the sands reclaimed this once lively and remarkable place for more than 3,000 years until its rediscovery by archaeologists in the 18th century.

Fig. 110. Paint brush. Excavators discovered this implement in the bedroom of House 1 in the Workmen's Village. Such brushes could be used for whitewashing the interiors of houses and tombs. UPMAA 2003-34-378. Amarna. Fiber and cordage. Length 16.5 cm (6.5 in) and width 5.4 cm (2.1 in).

Fig. 111. Comb. Excavators
found the comb in the front hall
of House 10 in the Workmen's
Village. Ancient hairstyles, especially women's, were often quite
elaborate, and the Egyptians
used combs for styling both natural hair and wigs worn by both
men and women. UPMAA 2003-
34-6. Amarna. Wood. Length
8.5 cm (3.3 in) and width 9.2 cm
(3.6 in).

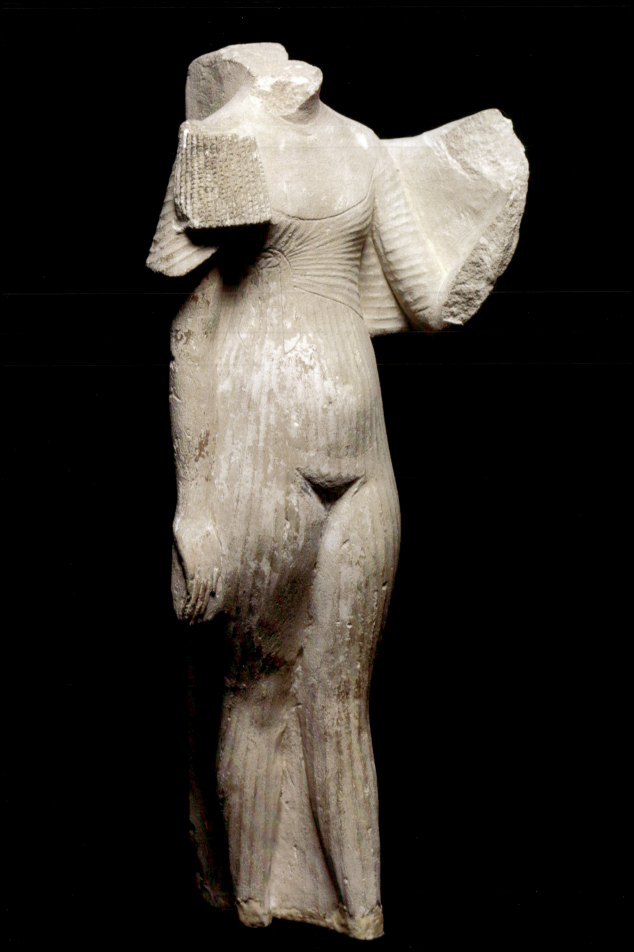

7

THE ROYAL WOMEN OF AMARNA

*B*eautiful in the Beauty of the Aten

Women in all levels of ancient Egyptian society enjoyed great-er freedoms and a closer equality with men than their counterparts in other contemporary ancient Near Eastern and Mediterranean cultures. The royal women of the New Kingdom (1539–1075 BCE) in particular are prominent in the historical record, assuming roles of consequence, beginning with Queen Ahhotep, who probably served as regent for her son, King Ahmosis, at the beginning of his reign and aided this founder of the 18th Dynasty in his struggles for independence from the Hyksos, the foreign kings who ruled Egypt for about 100 years during the Second Intermediate Period (1630–1539/23). Ahmosis's wife, Queen Ahmose-Nefertari, was the daughter of King Kamose, the last king of the 17th Dynasty. She too wielded considerable influence for almost 50 years during the reigns of her husband and later her son, Amenhotep I. This long-lived queen survived into the reign of Tuthmosis I. The ancient Egyptians established a posthumous cult for Ahmose-Nefertari in association with her son soon after her death. The later tomb builders of Deir el Medina established a cult for worship of Ah-most-Nefertari and her son, the founder of this city of necropolis workmen.

Later in the dynasty Queen Hatshepsut, another powerful woman, began her reign as regent for Tuthmosis III, a son of the deceased king by a minor wife. She soon assumed the status of full-fledged king. As king, Hatshepsut had herself depicted in male dress, and texts composed during this period often refer to her with masculine pronouns. She reigned as pharaoh for about 20 years before disappearing from the scene.

In keeping with this tradition, the women of the Amarna Period were equally influential and visible. It appears that more informa-tion is available about this group of royal women than for almost all the other queens and princesses of Egypt combined. Despite this seeming richness of knowledge, much scholarly debate exists about these women. Who were they? Where did they come from? Who were their children?

Fig. 112, opposite. Statue of Hatshepsut. Metropolitan Museum of Art 29.3.3. New York. Photo Courtesy of David P. Silverman. Granite. Height 167 cm (65.7 in).

Fig. 113. Fragments of two jar stoppers. Stoppers such as these originally sealed large vessels of wine. The fragment on left bears the name of an estate of Queen Tiye. The one on right names an estate of Amenhotep III. UPMAA 81-9-80. Amarna. Mud with pigment. Length 12 cm (4.7 in) and width 8.8 cm (3.5 in). UPMAA 81-9-82. Amarna. Length 16.4 cm (6.5 in) and width 8.6 cm (3.4 in).

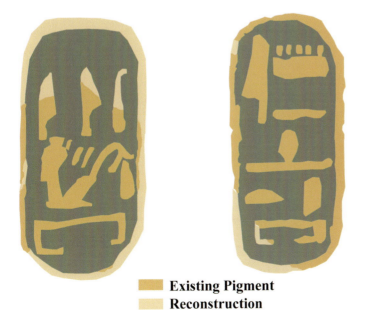

■ **Existing Pigment**
■ **Reconstruction**

Fig. 114. Reconstruction of jar stoppers.

A survey of the women of the Amarna Period begins with the reign of Akhenaten's father, Amenhotep III (see Figure 12). Like most Egyptian pharaohs Amenhotep III had numerous wives. One of these women, his primary wife, was the non-royal Tiye, who exerted considerable authority throughout the reigns of her husband and his successor, their son, Akhenaten (born Amenhotep IV). While non-royal Tiye's family lines were certainly not common. Military service and priestly duties closely associated her family with the throne. Queen Tiye's father, Yuya, held the priestly title "God's Father." He came from the town of Akhmim and served as the Commander of Chariotry. Her mother, Tjuya, was a priestess of the god Min. One of Queen Tiye's brothers, Anen, held an important position in the priesthood of Amun. Aye, the influential royal courtier during the reigns of Amenhotep III and Akhenaten, may also have been her brother, and it is he who would eventually succeed Tutankhamun as pharaoh. Since some scholars suggest that Aye was the father of Nefertiti, it is also possible that Nefertiti, the woman who married Tiye's son, was her niece.

Married at least by the second year of King Amenhotep III's reign, Queen Tiye's significance in his court became readily apparent. Monuments record Queen Tiye's presence at her husband's side, fulfilling both secular and religious roles, in a way unparalleled by previous Egyptian queens. For example, the full pharaonic titulary, the names and titles of the king used in monumental inscriptions, now incorporated her name. In addition to her high royal status, she was worshipped as a living form of the goddess Hathor at a temple in Sedeinga that her husband built in Nubia. In other temples worshippers identified Queen Tiye with several other goddesses including Maat and Taweret.

Amenhotep III and Queen Tiye had four daughters—Sitamun, Henut-taneb, Isis, and Nebet-ah, each of whom shared the title of Royal Wife with Queen Tiye. Their designation as their father's wife may have been a purely religious title, indicating that perhaps they served in place of their mother in some court functions or cult ceremonies. We have no evidence that any of them bore him children.

Queen Tiye's influence continued even after her husband's death. When her son, Akhenaten, moved the capital from Thebes to Amarna, Queen Tiye may have moved with him to the new city. Even if she did not make the move to Amarna permanently, she remained involved in political affairs. The continuing international esteem of the Queen Mother during the reign of her son is clear in one of the Amarna Letters (EA 26) in which the northern Mesopotamian Mitannian king, Tushratta, writes to her directly to complain that Akhenaten has not sent gifts of the same high quality that his father Amenhotep III had promised. Referring to the fact

Fig. 115. Illustration of the goddess Hathor.

that "gold is like dust in the country of your son," he ponders why she has not used her influence to ensure that her son Akhenaten would send large golden statuettes to him as pledged.

Queen Tiye made a special appearance at Amarna, receiving a pageant in her honor. Scenes from the Tomb of Huya at Amarna depict the royal couple, Akhenaten and Nefertiti, dining with Queen Tiye and show Akhenaten escorting Queen Tiye to the special sunshade temple erected in her honor. It is not clear if Tiye continued to stay at Amarna until her death around Year 14 of Akhenaten's reign, or even if she was buried in a tomb at Amarna.

Sarcophagus fragments with her name were found in the Royal Tomb at Amarna, and it is possible that she originally received burial at Amarna and that her mummy was later moved to Thebes after Amarna was abandoned. Since her husband had predeceased her, she would not have been interred in his tomb in the Valley of the Kings. Archaeologists found some of her funerary equipment in Tomb 55 (KV55) in the Valley of the Kings. Much debate has

Fig. 116. Illustration of the goddess Taweret.

focused on the identification of the body found with this material but scholars now accept that the body is that of a male. Robbers plundered Amenhotep III's tomb in antiquity, and priests reburied his mummy with other royal mummies in a cache in the tomb of Amenhotep II. A mummy called "The Elder Lady" was part of this group, and it is reasonable to suggest that this female mummy is that of Queen Tiye and that she ultimately found rest with her husband in this reburial. Analysis of hair from the mummy and a lock of hair found in a small anthropoid chest in the tomb of Tutankhamun seems to support this suggestion.

The most famous of all the Amarna women was Queen Nefertiti, the major wife of Akhenaten. While she is perhaps the most recognizable Egyptian queen, due in large part to the discovery of the exquisite painted bust of her, she remains an essentially mysterious figure. Her origins are unclear, and her name, meaning "The Beautiful One has Come," originally led scholars to suspect that she was a foreign princess sent as part of a diplomatic marriage to the Egyptian king. However, it may be more likely that her

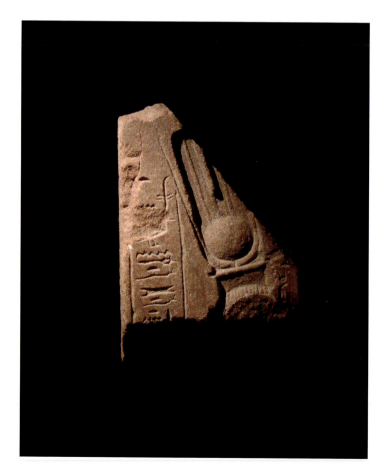

Fig. 117. Fragment of relief. One of the Amarna royal women wears an elaborate crown consisting of a sun disk, horns, and plumes, emphasizing her divine associations. UPMAA E664. Amarna. Granite. Height 15.5 cm (6.1 in), width 11 cm (4.3 in), and depth 7.5 cm (3 in).

Fig. 118. Scene of Queen
Tiye dining with Akhenaten and
Nefertiti, from the Tomb of Huya
at Amarna. After Davies (1905:
pl. VI).

father was Aye and that she, like Queen Tiye, originally came from
the town of Akhmim.

Akhenaten was probably already married to Nefertiti when he
came to the throne, and their marriage may have taken place when
both were still children. Regardless of her origins and relative
youth at the start of her husband's reign, it is clear that Queen
Nefertiti figured prominently in King Akhenaten's new religious
ideology from the beginning. Nefertiti appears in many representations in cult scenes where she can often stand as an equal
next to her husband.   A number of special prerogatives indicate
Nefertiti's preeminence among Akhenaten's wives. She is the only
one of his queens to have a full series of royal titles and epithets.
Only Nefertiti wears a royal crown and a *uraeus* at her brow. Only
Nefertiti and Akhenaten could experience special affection from
the Aten, in the form of receiving the *ankh* while the god caressed
them with his hands. It is interesting to note that despite her
seeming importance, Nefertiti's name, unlike that of Queen Tiye,
does not appear in the Amarna Letters.

Nefertiti remains prominent at Amarna until Year 12, when she
seems to disappear from the historical record. We do not know
the reason for her absence, but as seen earlier her eldest daughter,

Fig. 119. Sculptor's trial piece.   In this "artist's sketch" Nefertiti wears her tall flat-topped crown. Cairo Museum JE 59296. Photo courtesy of David P. Silverman. Limestone. Height 27 cm (10.6 in), width 16.5 cm (6.5 in), and depth 4 cm (1.6 in).

Fig. 120. Line drawing of Akhenaten, Nefertiti, and the Aten from the Tomb of Mahu at Amarna. After Davies (1906: pl. XV).

Meritaten, replaced her in the monumental record. Some scholars suggest that she neither disappeared nor died, but underwent a transformation to full coregent with her husband. Because of this new status, Nefertiti took the name Neferneferuaten, meaning, "Beautiful is the Beauty of the Aten." Her final resting place is unknown, but the text of Akhenaten's boundary stelae that he had set up at the edges of his city explicitly stated that he, Nefertiti, and his eldest daughter should be buried at the site. It is unclear if this command came to pass. After the Amarna Period, Nefertiti's images and texts mentioning her name were subject to the same deliberate destruction as those of her husband and his immediate successors.

As king Akhenaten appeared with women on virtually every representation of a cult-ritual or state ceremony that he conducted at Amarna. These women included a number of royal princesses. Of the nine princesses attested at Amarna, texts identify six of them specifically as the children of Akhenaten and Nefertiti. These royal daughters, in birth order, are Meritaten, Meketaten, Ankhsenpaaten, Neferneferuaten-Tasherit, Neferneferure, and Sete-

Fig. 121. Relief fragment. During the Amarna Period artists used a new style of representation reflecting aspects of the new theology. Occasionally they portrayed the king and other royal figures with exaggerated body features, such as swollen hips, rounded thighs, and elongated facial features, making it difficult sometimes to differentiate the king and queen. This royal head with a short wig may be either ruler. UPMAA 2006-13-1. Amarna. Red granite. Height 8.7 cm (3.4 in), width 8.0 cm (3.1 in), and depth 4.1 cm (1.6 in).

Fig. 122. Carved fragment. On one side of this corner fragment, which formed the edge of a stela or wall block, the artist shows a large royal figure (probably Nefertiti) standing in a pose of offering on one side. The other side shows the head of a princess holding a sistrum, a rattle-like musical instrument with religious associations. UPMAA 2006-13-2. Amarna. Quartzite. Height 19 cm (7.5 in), width 11 cm (4.5 in), depth 9 cm (3.5 in).

Fig. 123. Relief fragment. Part of Queen Nefertiti's body, as well as cartouches with her name, remains visible in this relief fragment. She typically appears behind Akhenaten at a slightly smaller scale. UPMAA E1007a. Amarna. Calcite. Height 11 cm (4.3 in), width 6.5 cm (2.6 in), and depth 10.7 cm (4.2 in).

penre.   Meritaten was probably born before Akhenaten came to the throne. She appears in reliefs, worshipping the Aten, where she usually follows her mother, Queen Nefertiti. Different numbers of her sisters occasionally accompany her. When Nefertiti disappeared around Year 12, Meritaten received the designation Chief Royal Wife.

Special mention should be made of the third daughter of Akhenaten and Nefertiti, Ankhsenpaaten. This royal princess was married at a young age to Prince Tutankhaten, who was perhaps her (half) brother. When Tutankhaten came to the throne, Ankhsenpaaten was elevated to queenly status. With the return to traditional beliefs, the young rulers changed their names to reflect the reestablishment of Amun as chief god in the pantheon. Ankhsenpaaten ("She Lives for the Aten") became Ankhsenamun ("She Lives for Amun") and Tutankhaten ("Perfect is the Life of Aten") became Tutankhamun (Perfect is the Life of Amun"). Ankhsenamun

Fig. 124. Statue of a princess. Amarna art placed considerable emphasis on the six daughters of Akhenaten and Nefertiti, though the name of this princess is not preserved. UPMAA E14349. Amarna. Limestone with pigment. Height 31.1cm (12.2 in), width 13 cm (5.1 in), and depth 10 cm (3.9 in).

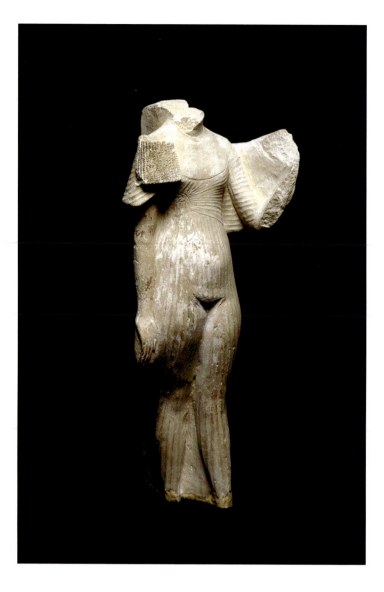

appears on many of her husband's monuments and on objects from his tomnb (see Figure 150).

With the premature death of her husband at the age of 19, Ankhsenamun found herself in what may have been a desperate situation. The Hittite annals record letters written by an anonymous Egyptian queen to the Hittite king in which the widowed queen asks the king to send his son to be her consort. While not named explicitly, Ankhsenamun may well have been that queen. Her efforts failed. The Hittite prince supposedly sent to Egypt disappeared on his journey, and so too does Ankhsenamun from the Egyptian historical record.

Fig. 125. Fragment of relief. The remnants of the scene depict a princess with a sistrum. E2208. Amarna. Granite. Height 19.3 cm (7.6 in), width 10.7 cm (4.2 in), and depth 6 cm (2.4 in).

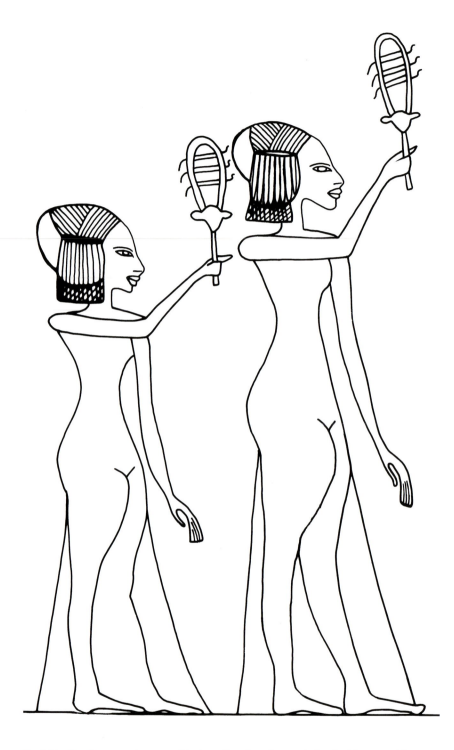

Fig. 126. Two Amarna princesses with sistra. Drawing after a relief in the Museum of Fine Arts Boston 1992.18.

Fig. 127. Section of relief. Part of a larger composition, this relief of Akhenaten with his daughter Meritaten originally decorated a sunshade temple dedicated to her at Amarna. The deeply carved bodies of the royal figures once contained inlay, probably in colored faience. After the Amarna Period artisans cut the original relief to its present size and shape, placed it face down, and reused the stone as the base of a sphinx of Pharaoh Merenptah of the 19th Dynasty. UPMAA E16230. Amarna. Quartzite. Height 232 cm (91.3 in), width 66 cm (26 in), depth 24 cm (9.4 in).

Both Akhenaten and his father Amenhotep III took part in diplomatic marriages with foreign princesses. King Shuttarna II sent one of these women, a Mitannian princess named Gilukhipa, to become a wife of Amenhotep III in the tenth year of his reign. Her niece, Tadukhipa, the daughter of King Tushratta, came to Egypt at the end of the reign of Amenhotep III. Tadukhipa became one of Akhenaten's wives after his father's death, and she continued to appear in the records until the fourth year of Akhenaten. Some scholars identify her as Kiya, a secondary wife of Akhenaten. Kiya is a mysterious figure who was not as

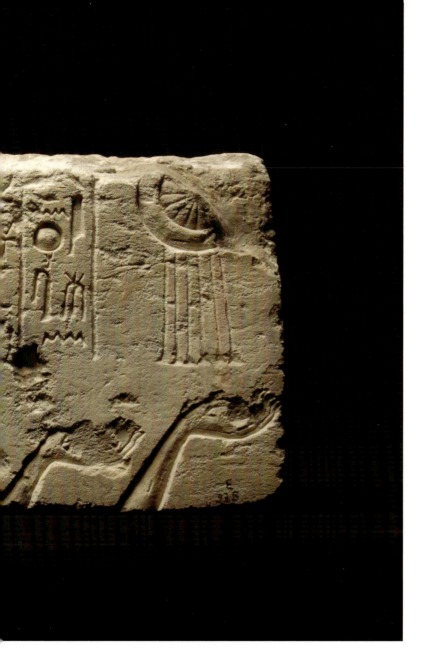

Fig. 128. Carved block. Akhenaten appears with two of his daughters. One, Ankhe-senpaaten, reaches toward an earring in the shape of the Aten. Scenes detailing royal family intimacy, common in Amarna art, may have had religious signifi-cance. UPMAA E325. Amarna. Limestone. Height 23 cm (9.1 in), width 56 cm (22 in), and depth 13 cm (5.1 in).

prominent as some of the other royal women. She did, however, receive special treatment at Amarna, such as the construction of her own chapels. It is interesting to note that she never appears in relief with Nefertiti. As wife to Akhenaten, Kiya seems to have born him at least one daughter, and it is possible that she was the mother of Tutankhamun.

The identification of the parentage of Tutankhamun is an on-going debate. The young prince does not appear in relief scenes and decoration in the way the young princesses do. No captions which might identify his mother and father exist. Tutankhamun's

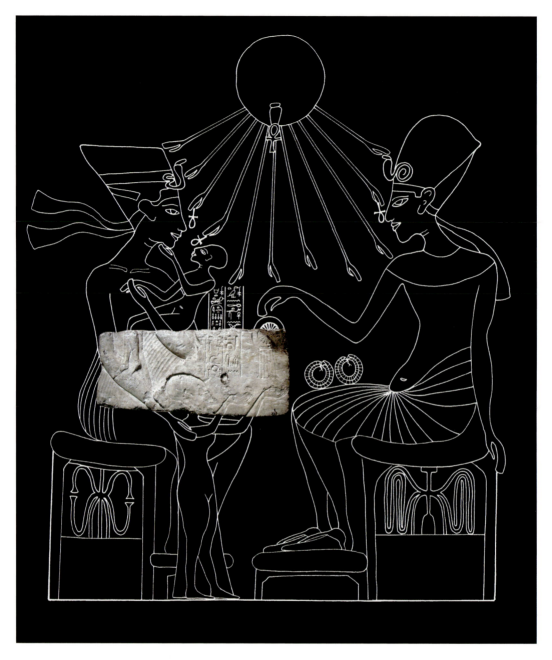

Fig. 129. Reconstructed scene of the royal family with E325 (Figure 128) in place.

Fig. 130. Canopic jar lid. The individual represented on this Egyptian alabaster jar may be one of the Amarna royal women--Queen Tiye, Nefertiti, Kiya, or Meritaten. The jar's inscription was originally for Kiya. Metropolitan Museum of Art 07.226.1. New York. Photo courtesy of David P. Silverman. Calcite. Height 37 cm (14.6 cm) and diameter 22 cm (8.7 in).

Fig. 131. Fragment from a statue group. Tutankhamun kneels before the god Amun, whom he restored to importance. All that remains of the god is his hand. The pharaoh wears the "war crown" or the "blue crown." Metropolitan Museum of Art 50.6. New York. Photo Courtesy of David P. Silverman. Indurated limestone. Height 15.2 cm (6 in.).

father may have been Amenhotep III, making him a younger (half) brother of Akhenaten, but it is equally possible that his father was Akhenaten or even Smenkhkare. His mother may have been Tiye, Nefertiti, or Kiya. Others suggest that either Princess Sitamun or Princess Meritaten may have been his mother. We believe that Tutankhamun grew up with the royal family at the city of Amarna and likely spent his younger years with these very important royal women.

The iconography in the sculpture and relief provides evidence of the high status of the remarkable women of the Amarna Period, appearing beside the king in a way not seen prior to this period in religious and ceremonial roles. Correspondence in the Amarna Letters attests to Queen Tiye's political significance and Ankhsenamun's important role. The beauty of these women is evident in the scores of representations that artists executed in relief and sculpture. The very names of Akhenaten's beloved wife, Nefertiti, or Neferneferuaten, celebrate her as a manifestation of the beauty of the Aten.

Fig. 132. Relief of a female figure. The royal woman wears a sheer pleated linen gown. Traces of a base or a platform under her feet indicate that the figure may have been a statue in a shrine. The curved lines are characteristic of the more naturalistic style artists used during the later parts of the Amarna Period. UPMAA E1007e. Amarna. Limestone with pigment. Height 26.5 cm (10.4 in), width 27 cm (10.6 in), and depth 7 cm (2.8 in).

8

EGYPT'S EMPIRE DURING THE AMARNA AGE

He Makes us Stand all Day in the Sun

By the time of the reign of Amenhotep III Egypt controlled a vast empire reaching from northern Syria to the fourth cataract of the Nile in Sudan. The 37-year reign of Amenhotep III was stable, and Egypt was incredibly wealthy thanks to years of relative peace, flourishing trade, and a continual cycle of tribute. Hostilities between Egypt and its former enemy, the Mitannian Empire, had been resolved during the reign of Tuthmosis IV, the father of Amenhotep III, who had married the daughter of the Mitannian king, Artatama I. Egypt was arguably the most important kingdom in the ancient world and was on good terms with the other influential leaders of the ancient Near East, such as the kings of Mitanni, Babylonia, Assyria, and the Hittites. Collectively known as the Great Kings, these rulers treated each other as equals and referred to each other as "brother."

In marked contrast to his predecessors, such as Tuthmosis III and Amenhotep II who undertook many battles in this region, Amenhotep III left no records of military campaigns in western Asia. He had inherited a prosperous and secure kingdom, and with the exception of military campaigns in Nubia in the early years of his reign, he relied more on skillful diplomacy than military threats to maintain his position. Amenhotep III and the other Great Kings seemed to recognize that peaceful interaction and the exchange of goods led to a mutually beneficial balance of power.

Much of our information about international relations during the Amarna Period comes from the Amarna Letters (EA), a group of about 350 documents of international royal correspondence, spanning roughly 30 years, from the 30th year of the reign of Amenhotep III until the early years of Tutankhamun. Written in cuneiform script, principally in Akkadian (the diplomatic language of the day), the letters are inscribed on sun-baked clay tablets. In 1887, a villager digging for ancient mudbrick to use as fertilizer accidentally uncovered this unique corpus at the site of Amarna.

The letters are both tantalizingly useful and undeniably frustrating. They offer a unique glimpse into the socio-political world

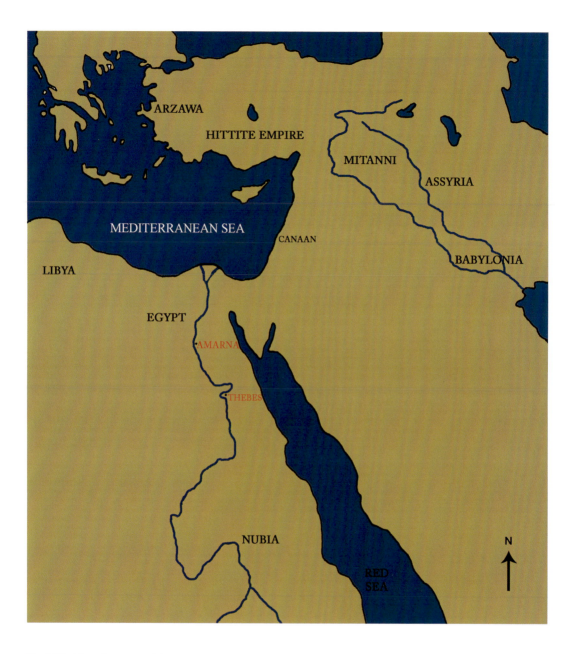

Fig. 133. Map of empires of the
ancient Near East.

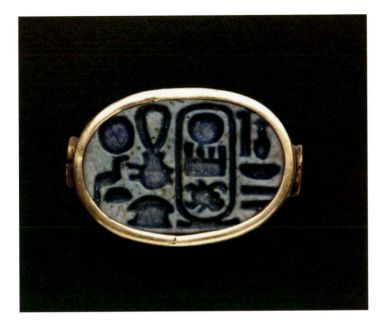

Fig. 134. Scarab of Tuthmosis III. UPMAA E13055. Glazed steatite. Height 2.2 cm (.8 in), width 1.58 cm (.6 in), and depth .95 cm (.7 in).

Fig. 135. Drawing of text on the scarab's base.

Fig. 136. Head of Amenhotep II. Possibly from a kneeling statue in a temple, this royal head's crown is too incomplete to determine its type. The king has the uraeus on his brow. His features appear similar to those on other statues of Amenhotep II. UPMAA E14304. Granodiorite. Height 17.5 cm (6.9 in), width 10.89 cm (4.3 in), and depth 16.59 cm (6.5 in).

of Egypt and the ancient Near East during the late 18th Dynasty, but they are often oblique, their translation difficult, and their chronology uncertain. We can categorize the letters into two general groupings. One focuses on communications among the contemporaries of the Egyptian pharaoh, the Great Kings, who deal with the Egyptian king on a roughly equal basis. The other is devoted to activities of the numerous vassals who were under the influence of the Great Kings.

In the first category, messages display the Egyptian king's desire to acquire foreign princesses. Diplomatic marriages were an important part of international relations at the time and helped to cement alliances with foreign rulers. Exchanges of lavish goods accompanied the brides in the form of raw materials as well as

Fig. 137. Commemorative scarab. Amenhotep III issued a series of items in honor of events during his reign. These eight lines of text describe lion hunts in the first ten years of his reign. UPMAA E21. Steatite. Length 8.3 cm (3.3 in) and width 5.3 cm (2.1 in).

finished products. For their part, the foreign kings are clearly quite interested in obtaining gold from Egypt. For example, in EA 43, the King of Babylon, Kadašman-Enlil I, enquires of Amenhotep III why he has not received an Egyptian princess to marry. Amenhotep III explained that no Egyptian princess had ever been sent abroad to become the wife of a foreign ruler. In his letter (EA 3), the King of Babylon notes that if the Egyptian king desires to marry one of his daughters, Amenhotep III would have to send a group to collect her and send more (and better) gold than he had sent previously.

The second group of letters concerns the subordinate standing of the vassal states. This correspondence contains effusively

Fig. 138. Bottom of scarab.
UPMAA E21.

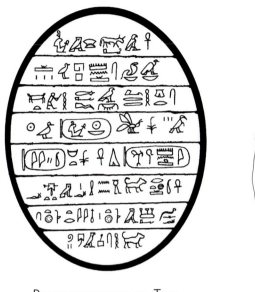

RECONSTRUCTION OF TEXT   LION HUNT SCARAB (E21)

Fig. 139. Reconstruction of the text of the Lion Hunt scarab.

humble pledges of loyalty to the Egyptian king and repetitive requests for aid. For example in EA 299, the ruler of Gaza refers to himself as "your servant, the dirt at your feet, the groom of your horses." He pleads with the king: "<g>ive me his help, and may the king, my lord get me away from the Apiru lest the Apiru destroy us."

Under Amenhotep III Egyptian control of Syro-Palestine was divided into three areas, each of which had its own Egyptian governor. The governor based at Gaza was responsible for "Canaan" (the area now including modern Israel, Palestine, Jordan, and the Lebanese coast as far as Beirut); the governor at Kumidu (in Lebanon) was in charge of the area, which stretches to Syria, while a third governor in Simurru (in Syria) oversaw "Amurru," the coastal lands north to Ugarit. The Egyptian governor was charged with ensuring that the local rulers remained loyal to Egypt. These vassals sent tribute to Egypt in exchange for the right to remain in power and were responsible for supplying the military garrisons in their areas. The Amarna Letters report that these local rulers

Fig. 140. Jar stopper. The impression on this jar stopper bears the prenomen of Amenhotep III, Nebmaatre. Stoppers served as seals for vessels. UPMAA 81.9.190. Mud. Diameter 20 cm (7.9 in).

occasionally wrote to the Egyptian king requesting more troops when squabbles arose between their neighbors.

The majority of this correspondence dates to the reign of Akhenaten, and he inherited an increasingly complicated international situation concerning two of Egypt's neighboring kingdoms. The Mitannian King, Tushratta, and the Hittite king, Suppiluliuma, frequently wrote to Akhenaten. In one letter (EA 29) from Tushratta to Akhenaten, the Mitannian king greets the pharaoh and sends good wishes to him as well as to his daughter, Tadukhipa, a Mitannian princess originally dispatched to Egypt as a bride for

Fig. 141. Line drawing of the stopper.

Amenhotep III and whom his son Akhenaten consequently "inherited."

A letter (EA 41) from the Hittite king hints at what might be a treaty between himself and Akhenaten. It is similar to the missive from the Mitannian king in also referring to past relationships between Egypt and the Hittite kingdom and requests aid: "The messages I sent to your father and the wishes he expressed to me will certainly be renewed between us. O King, I did not reject anything your father asked for, and your father never neglected any of the wishes I expressed, but

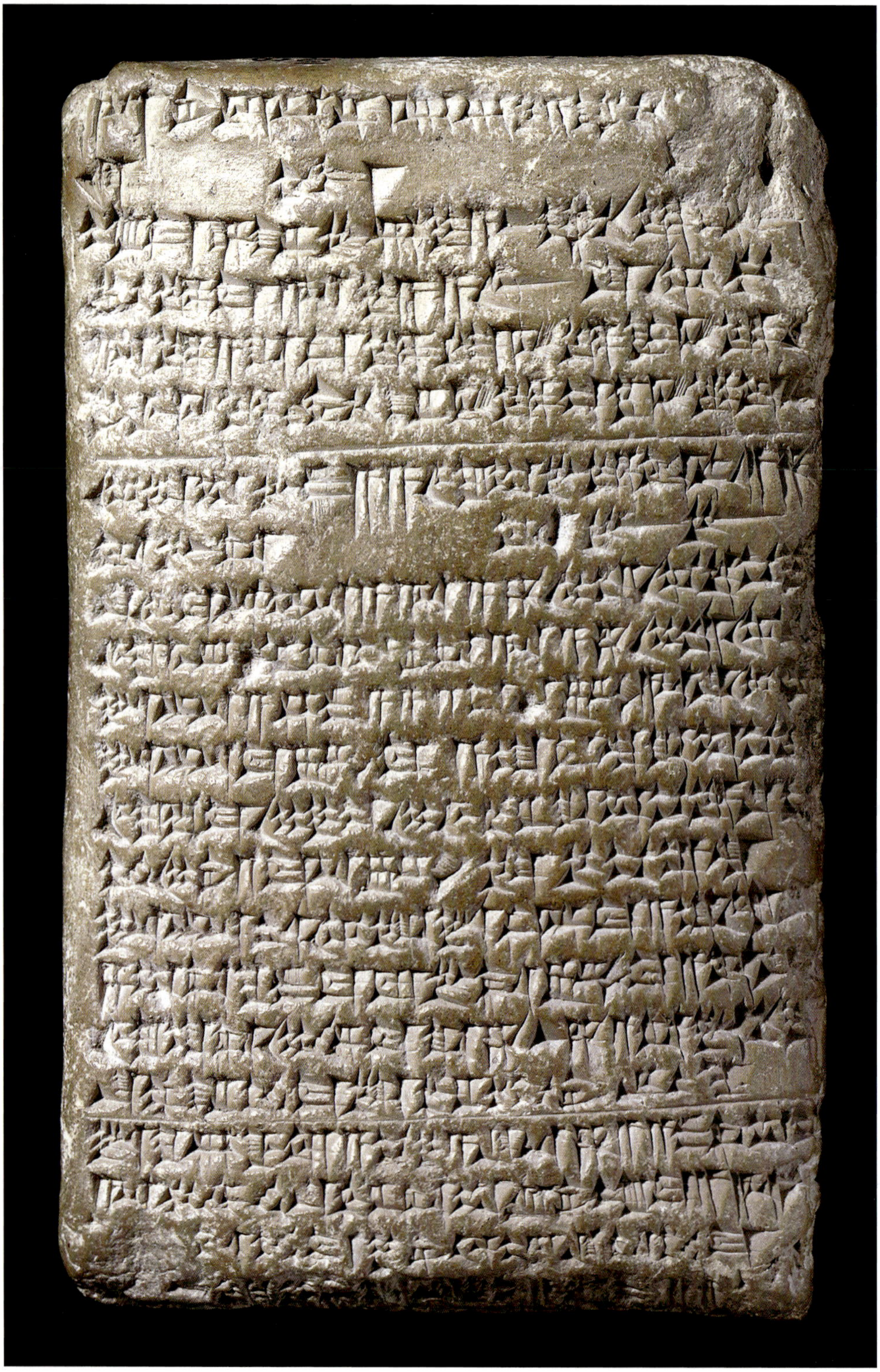

Fig. 142. An Amarna letter written on a clay tablet addressed to Akhenaten/Amenhotep IV from Burnabur-rias, a king of the Kassite dynasty in Babylonia, who complains here that the gifts Akhenaten sends him are not valuable enough. ANE E29785. Photo © Trustees of The British Museum.

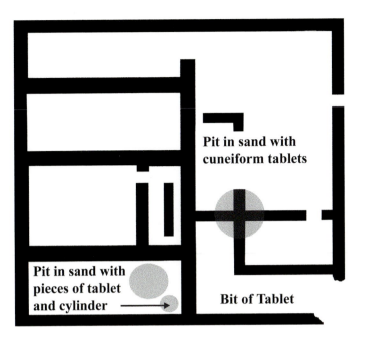

Fig. 143. Plan of find spot of the letters excavated at Amarna by Flinders Petrie in 1891–92. Drawn after Petrie (1894:pl. XLII.19).

granted me everything. Why have you, my brother, refused to send me what your father during his lifetime has sent me?"

The hostilities between the Hittite empire, based in Anatolia, and the Mitannian Empire, based in northern Mesopotamia, erupted into a full-scale war during the reign of Akhenaten. The kingdom of Mitanni, a longstanding Egyptian ally, came under increasing pressure from the Hittites. During Tushratta's reign, Suppiluliuma destroyed Washukkani, the capital city of the Mitanni, and Tushratta was assassinated in the subsequent chaos. Tushratta's successor, Artatama, abandoned hope for Egyptian aid and made an alliance with the Assyrians instead.

In addition to their conflicts with the Mitanni, the Hittites were also stirring up instability in the vassal states of Syria, and a nomadic group, the Apiru, was creating unrest in Syro-Palestine. Egypt's other allies who attempted to rebel against the Hittites were captured, and they wrote to Akhenaten begging for troops; he evidently did not respond to their pleas. In addition, many vassal rulers requested gold from the pharaoh and complained that he ignored them or cheated them.

Whereas earlier, more military-minded New Kingdom pharaohs would have settled these conflicts with a decisive campaign, Akhenaten, it seems, was content to keep the status quo of establishing garrisons throughout Egypt's territorial possessions, dealing with each of the vassals as necessary. Some modern scholars

criticize Akhenaten, noting that he focused all of his efforts on his religious ideas and thereby allowed Egypt's international prestige to deteriorate. This failure to act resolutely on international matters resulted in a dangerous situation for Egypt, as the Hittites soon became a major threat to Egyptian control of Syro-Palestine. The rise of the Hittite empire continued to plague Egyptian kings at the end of the 18th Dynasty and erupted into full-scale war at the beginning of the 19th Dynasty, resolved only during the reign of Ramses II.

Fig. 144, opposite. Peace treaty of Ramses II with the Hittites. Ramses II had a relief carved near the colossal royal figures that fronted his temple at Abu Simbel to commemorate his treaty. Photo Courtesy of David P. Silverman.

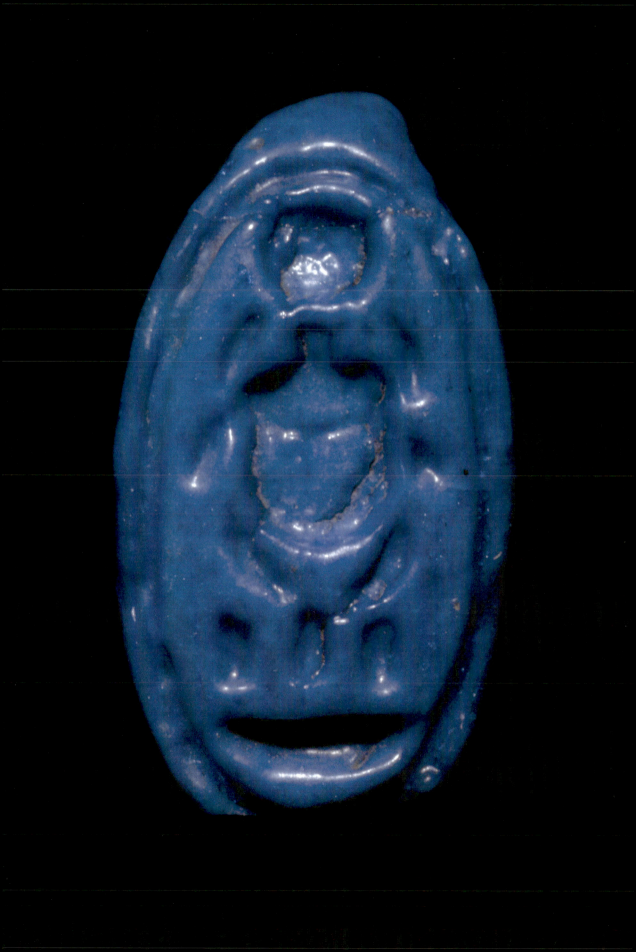

9

TUTANKHAMUN AND THE RETURN TO TRADITION

From Elephantine to the marshes of the Delta, temples of the gods and goddesses had fallen into neglect, and shrines had become desolated

Tutankhamun had these words inscribed on a stela he erected in the hypostyle court of the temple of Amun at Karnak. He claimed to have found Egypt in a ruinous state when he "appeared as king," according to this inscription, but he had actually come to the throne several years earlier during a period of reconciliation. His words are more a reflection of his break with Atenist beliefs than a narration of historical events. He uses only his later name, Tutankhamun, and provides no reference to his earlier life at Amarna, where he called himself Tutankhaten. There is no account of the apparent problems that arose with the succession after the death of Akhenaten around 1336 BCE. For the young king, it is as if this short interval of three to four years did not exist.

Ancient records are not clear as to who directly succeeded Akhenaten, but perhaps as many as four years elapsed before Tutankhamun came to the throne in 1332 BCE. One or two other pharaohs may have had brief reigns before him. Smenkhkare, an apparent coregent of Akhenaten, may have been an older brother of Tutankhamun, or even his father, with perhaps even a short independent rule. Nefertiti, Akhenaten's queen, appears to have been the other. Questions as to whether both individuals actually ruled, and if so, in what order they reigned, remain unsolved. Part of the confusion arises over the use of the throne name Ankhkheperure. Both Smenkhkare and Nefertiti (when she used the personal name Neferneferuaten) appear to have employed this same identification. Because of the ambiguity, scholars have not agreed upon which individual(s) served as king from 1336 to 1332 BCE.

Inscriptions with both names seem to indicate that a period of reconciliation existed between adherents of the Aten and of the traditional religion, with Amun at its head. Texts mainly from Amarna, but a few from Thebes, with the names of these rulers once again refer to the gods of the pantheon, yet there is no evidence of overt suppression of the Aten. Amun was regaining his former importance, and priesthoods at temples throughout the land began to function again.

Fig. 145. Restoration stele of Tutankhamun. The pharaoh had this stela erected in the Temple of Amun at Karnak to record his restoration of the traditional gods that his probable father had abandoned. Cairo Museum JE 43183. Quartzite. Height 129 cm (50.8 in). Photograph after P. Lacau, CCG no. 34183 (1909:pl. 70).

Fig. 146. Golden canopic coffinette from the tomb of Tutankhamun. One of four vessels for the mummified internal organs of the king, this one originally held his liver. Inscriptions cover the exterior and interior of this container, and traces of earlier hieroglyphs near the royal name indicate that Tutankhamun was not the original owner. Cairo Museum Carter 266g. Photo courtesy of David P. Silverman. Gold, carnelian, obsidian, rock crystal, and glass. Height 10 cm (3.9 in), width 11 cm (4.3 in), and length 39.5 cm (15.6 in).

Fig. 149. Royal crook from the tomb of Tutankhamun. Usually coupled with the flail, the crook is one of the two emblems of Egyptian kingship that the king held. When written as a hieroglyph, the crook (heqa) meant "ruler." The name Tutankhaten occurs on the base cap. Cairo Museum Carter 269h. Photo courtesy of David P. Silverman. Gold, glass, copper alloy, wood, and carnelian. Length 43.3 cm (17 in) and width 10.2 cm (4 in).

Fig. 150, opposite. Throne from the Tomb of Tutankhamun. This detail from his back of the throne portrays Tutankhamun and Ankhsenamun below the rays of the Aten. Cairo Museum JE 62028. Photo courtesy of David P. Silverman. Wood, gold, glass, and semiprecious stones. Height 104 cm (40.9 in), width 53 cm (20.9 in), and depth 65 cm (25.6 in).

rna style, appears on its back. The Aten floats above the couple, extending its lifegiving rays toward them. Both the earlier name Tutankhaten, and the later, Tutankhamun, appear on the throne, but the latter seems to receive more prominent locations in inscriptions. The use of both names on the single item suggests that at least for a period of time during the reign of the young king the two religions existed without apparent conflict. Such information suggests that Tutankhaten likely spent several years on the throne in the city that his probable father, Akhenaten, had built to glorify his new god.

Tutankhaten eventually began to expand the reconciliation with traditional ideology, introduced before he came to the throne.

Fig. 151. Statue of Amun. Amun usually takes the form of a human male, here wearing the false beard of a deity, an elaborate broad collar, and a short kilt decorated on the belt with a tyet-amulet, a symbol related both to Isis and to the hieroglyph ankh. The god also holds the same sign in each hand, indicating his immortality. Sculptors intentionally cut back his hands to allow the statue to fit into a shrine or a portable ceremonial boat. UPMAA E14350. Greywacke, gilt. Height 45.4 cm (17.9 in), width 15.23 cm (6 in), and depth 13.33 cm (5.3 in).

Fig. 152, opposite. Statue of the goddess Amunet from Karnak. Tutankhamun had many statues of traditional gods set up in the Temple of Amun. Among them were the figures of Amun and Amunet, his consort, whose image resembled his wife, Ankhsenamun. Photo courtesy of David P. Silverman.

Fig. 153. View of the site of Amarna today. Photo courtesy of Kenneth Garrett.

In addition to assuming the name Tutankhamun, he recorded the "restoration" inscription, a very small part of which is quoted in the epigraph to this chapter. But did his account accurately record the state of Egypt after the reign of Akhenaten and for how much of the "restoration" could he in fact take responsibility?

Answers to these questions lie in part in the understanding of the purpose of this type of inscription for the ancient Egyptians. Its form is not unique; other pharaohs before Tutankhamun had set up similar texts, ordinarily early in their reign. Some scholars have suggested that the damaged introduction in Tutankhamun's text would originally have listed the year of its composition as the first of his reign. Given the use of the later form of his name on the stela and its location in Thebes, in a temple devoted to the god Amun, it clearly was erected later, perhaps to mark his return to the traditional religious capital. He may have wanted to indicate this time as the real beginning of his rule, and for this reason recorded the date as Year 1 of his reign.

Fig. 154, opposite. Royal kneeling figure. The statue's modified broad hips, heavy thighs, and elongated facial features indicate that it belongs to the latter part of the Amarna Period. The face resembles that of Tutankhamun as seen on some of his other monuments. It represents part of an implement that served a ritual purpose in the temple. When complete, this royal figure would have knelt before a deity. The headdress and chest contain traces of gold, and the eyes and eyebrows were originally inlaid. UPMAA E14295. Black bronze with gold. Height 22.86 cm (9 in), width 10.16 cm (4 in), and depth 15.24 cm (6 in).

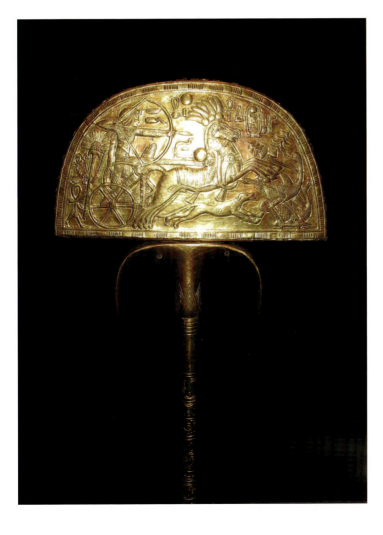

Fig. 155. Golden fan from the tomb of Tutankhamun. Scenes on both sides of the fan portray the king in a chariot, a type that may be also used in military activities. Several chariots and different types of weaponry were interred with Tutankhamun. Cairo Museum 62001. Photo courtesy of David P. Silverman. Gilded wood. Length of fan 105.5 cm (41.3 in) and width of palm 18.5 cm (7.3 in).

Fig. 156. Wall scene from the Tomb of Tutankhamun. Standing on the right Aye wears a blue crown and a priestly robe, performing the funerary rite of "opening the mouth" on the mummiform figure of Tutankhamun on the left. Photo courtesy of David P. Silverman.

While on the surface, the king appears to have recorded "facts" on the stela, information presented on it also had other levels of interpretation. For Tutankhamun, it was a statement for eternity, placed in a Theban temple that itself functioned as a residence for the god Amun. As a sacred dwelling for deities, this structure represented the cosmos, and, like its divine inhabitants, it was meant for eternity. Moreover, the text was recorded in hieroglyphs, "god's words," in ancient Egyptian, also sacred and eternal. What the signs recorded, therefore, was meant as everlasting truth.

Although only a few people would have immediate access to the temple enclosure and the stele within its court, the presence of the inscription in a sacred setting was of critical importance to

Fig. 157. Statue of Akhenaten. This statue of a king depicts the pharaoh seated on a cushion, wearing a royal nemes crown and holding the crook and flail. The more naturalistic features, pronounced curves, swollen belly, and pierced ears suggest a date in the Amarna Period, perhaps Akhenaten. The figure has no identifying inscriptions. Musée du Louvre N831. Yellow stone. Photo courtesy of David P. Silverman. Height 64 cm (25 inches), width 17.2 cm (6.7 inches), and depth 35 cm (13.8 inches).

ensure its longevity. Literate priests could recite the contents of the inscription to a larger portion of society during festivals and thus publicize the pharaoh's greatness among his subjects.

In addition to its propagandistic aspect for his contemporaries, it would also stand as a testament for future generations to learn about what had happened during his reign. Some events appear exaggerated, but others are omitted. There is no mention of what appears to have been a fairly peaceful period of reconciliation during the early years of his reign when he still resided at Amarna. Tutankhamun wanted to be remembered for the following: his rebuilding of the temples and shrines that he found in ruins, his reestablishment of the traditional deities whom he stated had forgotten humankind, and his bringing back the rituals, offerings, and prayers that sustained the deities.

Another purpose of the text on the stela was to legitimize Tutankhamun's right to rule. On a cosmic level his actions symbolically portrayed him in the role of a creator god who was bringing order to a chaotic universe. He was acting according to maat, reinstating the balance necessary for the universe to function. Neither the erection of the stela nor the message it related were unique to this king. The events that some pharaohs recorded were closer to the truth—for example, that on the stela of Kamose of the 17th Dynasty (1543-1539 BCE), which narrated his battle against the

Fig. 158, opposite. Relief of Horemheb from Luxor. Tutankhamun had this scene carved on the wall of the Temple of Amun at Luxor, showing him offering to the god. The text originally identified him as officiant. Horemheb appropriated this scene and other monuments by replacing the name of his predecessor with his own. Photo courtesy of David P. Silverman.

Fig. 159. King list from Abydos. From the 19th Dynasty temple of Seti I at Abydos, this relief records the known kings who ruled Egypt, but with no names of any of the Amarna Period kings. Horemheb had effectively removed them from public memory. Photo courtesy of David P. Silverman.

Fig. 160. Howard Carter in
Tomb of Tutankhamun, 1922.
Photo by Harry Burton, expedition
photographer.

enemy Hyksos. Some, however, were further from the truth, such
as the essentially invented text that Hatshepsut (1749?-1458 BCE)
had inscribed. Whatever the content of the text, the inscription
stood as a symbol of the right of the pharaoh to rule as an incarna-
tion of the creator god.

A youth not yet in his teens at his accession, Tutankhamun was
too young to have participated in either the planning or the carrying out of most military activities. Scenes on a chest from his tomb
portray him in battles that, although mainly symbolic, may reflect
his interest in such pursuits.   His tomb contained a good deal of
military equipment, including chariots and weaponry, and he may
have used these items in life. Other related articles clearly served
in rituals or were meant for the afterlife. Several of Tutankhamun's
ancestors had recorded their physical and military prowess, and
he may have inherited such abilities.

Tutankhmaun died around the age of 19, and the actual cause of his death remains a mystery. X-rays taken in the latter part of the 20th century suggested that he might have received a fatal blow to the back of the head. This information led to speculation about his murder at the hands of one of his two successors. In 2005, the National Geographic Society arranged for CT scans to be done on Tutankhamun's mummy. They revealed that the dark area at the back of the skull that others had mistakenly assumed was a deliberate skull fracture was actually a consequence of the mummification process in the 18th Dynasty. The tests did show an unhealed injury to his left femur, or thighbone. This wound could have occurred just prior to his death and may have resulted from an accident. Since no signs of healing are evident, a related infection may have led to his death.

Fig. 161. Mirror case from the tomb of Tutankhamun. This gilded case in the shape of an *ankh* ("life") originally held a mirror, probably of a precious metal, that was stolen in antiquity. Cairo Museum JE 62349. Photo courtesy of David P. Silverman. Wood, gold, semiprecious stones, and glass. Height 27 cm (10.6 in).

Fig. 162. The god Nefertem from the tomb of Tutankhamun. This figure represents the young king as one of the traditional gods he had restored after he came to the throne. The youthful features of Nefertem may reflect both the god's role as a young sun god as well as Tutankhamun's youth. Cairo Museum JE 60723. Photo courtesy of David P. Silverman. Wood, plaster, and paint. Height 30 cm (11.8 in).

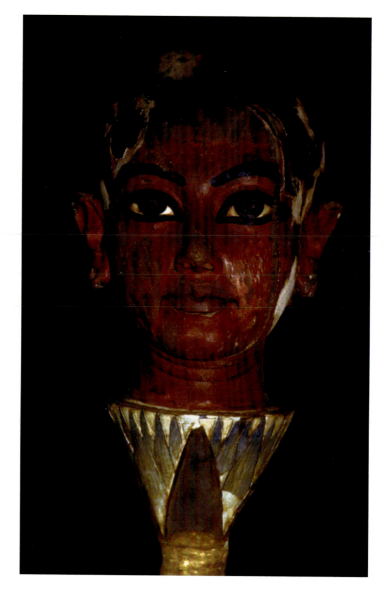

What happened to his wife, Ankhesenamun, after his death also remains a mystery. One of Akhenaten's, daughters, she played an important role in her husband's rule and frequently appeared alongside him in carved and painted scenes. She apparently survived him, but her tomb still awaits discovery.

In order to understand who eventually took over the throne of Egypt, it is necessary to look at the individuals in Tutankhamun's court who functioned as his advisors. Aye, the elderly court official and commander of chariotry, clearly stands out, and he ultimately succeeded Tutankhamun after the young king's untimely death. In Tutankhamun's tomb, it is Aye who conducted the ritual of the "Opening of the Mouth" for the dead king. Ordinarily it was the

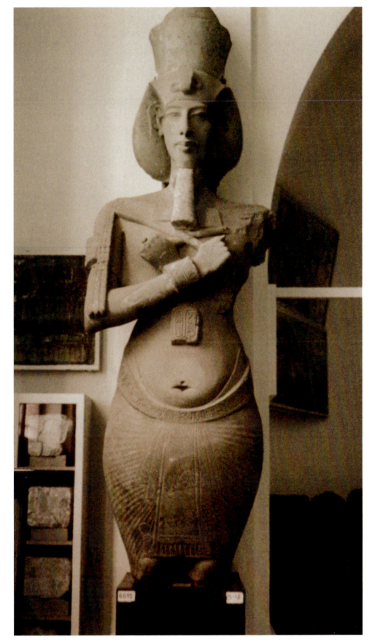

Fig. 163. Colossal statue of Akhenaten in the exaggerated style typical of his early reign. Numerous statues of Akhenaten in this style decorated the temples built at Karnak before the king founded Amarna. Excavated by Henri Chevrier in 1925. Cairo Museum JE 559,38. Photo courtesy of David Silverman. Sandstone. Original height approximately 4 meters (13ft).

heir, usually the son or heir who would perform the duty of re-animating the deceased, and Aye's appearance here suggests the great power he wielded during the reign of his young predecessor. Despite nonroyal birth, he had a burial on a royal scale in the Valley of the Kings, in a tomb perhaps originally designed for Tutankhamun. His advanced age and his short reign of three years prevented extensive advances in the restoration program. Surviving inscriptions indicate his inclusion of primarily traditional

Fig. 164. Relief with cartouches of Akhenaten. Shortly after the reign of Tutankhamun, the reaction against Akhenaten took hold much more deeply and resulted in the near-complete disman-tling of the monuments built for the Aten. The vast majority of stone elements, like this column fragment bearing Akhenaten's name, were removed to hide the memory of Akhenaten's reign. Ironically, the dismantling and reuse of these items managed to preserve them for posterity. UP-MAA E648A. Amarna. Limestone with pigment. Height 28 cm (11 in.) Width 30 cm (11.8 in) Depth 10 cm (3.9 in).

gods, but they do not suggest that he began any destruction of earlier monuments. Aye does refer to a war with the Hittite empire, Egypt's enemy from an area in modern Turkey, and it is likely that his military experience served him well both during Tutankhamun's reign and later during his own short rule.

Upon Aye's death, Horemheb, who had already served as a military officer during the latter part of Tutankhamun's reign and eventually became a general, emerged as pharaoh. His experience in battle, his knowledge of foreign affairs, and his familiarity with the royal court made him quite formidable. With no blood link to the royalty of the past, however, and no heir to carry on his line, his rule marked the end of the succession of kings descended from Tuthmosis III. Perhaps more important was his role in completing the restoration of orthodoxy and guiding Egypt back to a signifi-cant position among nations in the ancient Near East.

Horemheb also bears responsibility for nearly eradicating the Amarna heresy from Egypt's history. While he spent a good deal of his time on diplomatic, foreign, military, and economic issues, he also devoted much of his 27-year reign to removing traces of

Akhenaten, anyone related to him, and any link to the heretical years.

His program did not stop with Akhenaten and the Amarna experience. Under the command of Horemheb even Tutankhamun was not spared. The reigning pharaoh appropriated his predecessor's monuments and statues and reinscribed most of his texts for himself. It was not an innovation for a new king to take over some of the monuments of a predecessor; it was almost a privilege of the office of kingship. Horemheb, however, was fairly thorough in removing Tutankhamun's name and then also that of Aye from most monuments, perhaps in part for political reasons. As a non-royal figure ascending to the throne, he may have had concerns about his own legitimacy as ruler. He may also have been motivated because the reconciliations they had negotiated had not gone far enough for the people of Egypt who may have desired a complete split from the Akhenaten's radical theology.

By the 19th dynasty, when king lists record the register of pharaohs who ruled Egypt, the names of those related to the Amarna years—Akhenaten, Smenkhkare, Neferneferuaten, Tutankhamun, and Aye—are absent. Some 3,000 years later, however, an intrepid British archaeologist, Howard Carter, convinced himself that the tomb of Tutankhamun existed and that he could find it. Never giving up hope, he finally met success in 1922, when he discovered the final resting place of the young boy still sealed, holding the magnificent treasures with which he was buried for eternity.

Epilogue
The Modern Discovery of Amarna

After nearly 3,500 years, archaeology has succeeded in resurrecting the image of the once-despised revolutionary Pharaoh Akhenaten. The story of the rediscovery of Akhenaten by the modern world is every bit as intriguing as the short reign of this enigmatic pharaoh. Modern interest in Akhenaten includes fascination with the identity of this king who has sometimes been considered the world's first monotheist. It is also the story of the painstaking results of archaeological excavation and detective work which continues to this day, even as numerous mysteries and unanswered questions persist in the study of the Amarna Period.

Egyptologists and scholars of the 19th century were intrigued, although largely baffled by the strange image of Akhenaten. Khu-en-Aten—as they frequently wrote his name at that time—was noted for departing radically from the familiar styles of representation of Egyptian pharaohs. Nineteenth century images of Akhenaten, such as a famous scene in the Theban tomb of Ramose, vizier under Amenhotep III, contributed to the notion that Akhenaten suffered from a physical abnormality or was weak and effeminate. One scholar, Eugène Lefébvre, speculated that Akhenaten was not a man but a woman—similar to the earlier Hatshepsut—who had declared herself to be king. The eminent French Egyptologist Auguste Mariette hypothesized that Akhenaten may have been a eunuch, castrated after being captured during a military campaign in Nubia.

This view gradually changed later in the century when more evidence came to light and a greater appreciation for the nuances of the artistic style of the Amarna Age developed. Particularly important in this process was the clearance and initial recording of the badly damaged rock-cut tombs at Tell el-Amarna. Work on the tombs first occurred early in the 19th century. The first published record of the tombs is that of Richard Lepsius (published in 1847). Documentation of some of the city's boundary stelae around this same time added a set of crucial inscriptions that shed light on the reign of Akhenaten. Between 1902 and 1907, the British Egypt Exploration Fund undertook a comprehensive recording of the private tomb chapels at Amarna. The full publication of these ornately decorated tomb chapels still provides the most detailed window we have on the reign of Akhenaten and life in his capital city.

By the last decade of the 19th century Egyptologists had long been aware that the region in Middle Egypt of the modern villages of *et-Till* and *Beni Amaran* (origin of the modern name Tell el-Amarna) was the location of the ancient city named *Akhetaten*. No one, however, had yet initiated serious archaeological work on its physical remains. A major impetus to begin excavation at the site occurred in 1887, when a local village woman who was digging in the ancient ruins of Amarna for *sebakh* (organic fertilizer that Egyptian farmers once dug out of ancient sites) came upon a cache of clay tablets inscribed in mysterious writing. This was the famed discovery of the Amarna Letters which derive from the House of Royal Correspondence in the Central City of Amarna.

These tablets, inscribed in Akkadian, made scholars curious about the potential for major new discoveries of Akhenaten's reign through excavating the denuded ruins of his capital. The British archaeologist Flinders Petrie undertook the first substantial excavation work at Amarna during 1891–92. Petrie's brief period at Amarna revealed some of the major components of the central city and adjacent areas. Petrie's work contributed significant objects to a number of museums and institutions supporting his work, including the University of Pennsylvania Museum. One of Petrie's famous discoveries at Amarna was the magnificent painted pavements from part of the Great Palace which he designated the "harim." For many years those pavements were a tourist attraction at the site. Visitors on steamers sailing up the Nile would disembark to see these vibrant 3,500-year-old floors. Eventually an enraged farmer, tired of the visitors walking through his fields, attacked the floors. The Egyptian Antiquities Service rescued the remaining fragments, still impressive, and transported them to Cairo, where they stand today under glass in the grand central hall of the Egyptian Museum.

The German mission in Egypt, the Deutsche Orientgesellschaft, directed by Ludwig Borchardt, established the standard for archaeological investigation at Amarna. Between 1907 and 1914, the German expedition focused excavation efforts on the residential sectors of the city, particularly the extensive South Suburb and Main City with its combination of large mansions in walled compounds and smaller housing areas. The best-known discovery of this period is the house of the royal sculptor Thutmose, with a cache of plaster busts and images of the city's royalty and elite. The identity of many of the persons in these sculptures is unknown, but Egyptologists are uniformly certain on the identification of the striking bust of a queen, now in Berlin, as the image of Akhenaten's chief queen, Nefertiti (see Figure 17). Perhaps more than any other single object, this renowned royal image has inspired interest in the Amarna period and in the identity of Akhenaten's equally enigmatic queen.

During 1921–36, the British resumed work at Amarna spon-sored by the Egypt Exploration Fund. The scope of work during these years was considerable, with excavation of vast tracts of the Central City, the North Suburb, the North City, the *Maruaten*, Eastern Village (workmen's village), and other sites. While never rewarded with a find as stunning as the Nefertiti bust, the British excavations fleshed out the physical structure of Akhenaten's capi-tal. Archaeologists now largely understood the city's overall design and the functions of many of its constituent elements. The British at that time perhaps came the closest to living the experience of the Amarna Age since during their excavations of the North City they repaired one of the large well-preserved houses in that part of Amarna and used it as their dig house.

Between the two world wars both scholarly and popular inter-est in the Amarna Period increased yet further due to the 1922 discovery of the nearly intact tomb of Akhenaten's probable son, Tutankhamun. Although the image of Tutankhamun did not sug-gest the compelling mystery of his father, his rich burial goods in the Valley of the Kings, combined with echoes of the Amarna Age in his personal possessions, added to the allure of this unique period of the 18th Dynasty. The beautiful golden throne of Tut-ankhamun, still bearing the image of the Aten and that of the boy king and his queen Ankhesenamun, formerly the princess Ankhe-senpaaten, provide an intimate glimpse into the flavor of royal life at the end of the Amarna Period (see Figure 150).

After a lengthy hiatus in work at Amarna during World War II, excavations of the Egypt Exploration Society resumed in 1979 un-der the direction of Barry Kemp and continue to the present day. Amarna, like many of Egypt's ancient sites, is increasingly pres-sured by modern population growth and development along the edge of the Nile Valley. The renewed program of work has reexam-ined some of the previously studied sites and refined our under-standing of the history of the site. The new work has also revealed previously unknown buildings such as a new royal cult building at an isolated site called Kom el-Nana. While excavations at Amarna itself may not radically add to current evidence on the king him-self, the study of his capital city continues to be refined.

Over the years of the city's excavation between 1891 and 1936, the image of Akhenaten himself had changed considerably. The sense of mystery and near revulsion at his unorthodox appear-ance we saw in the 19th century had been replaced by a new view based on an appreciation for the ambitious extent of Akhenaten's religious revolution. Akhenaten tends to be seen now as a phi-losopher king, a prophet, and history's first individual. His religion was seen as a precursor to, if not the first manifestation of mono-theism. The historian James Breasted typified this conception of Akhenaten, writing in 1909, "There died with him such a spirit as the world had never seen before, a brave soul, undauntedly facing the momentum of immemorial tradition and thereby stepping out from the long line of conventional and colorless pharaohs."

These appraisals of Akhenaten have been tempered over the decades as scholars have increasingly understood some of the origins and motivations behind Akhenaten's religious revolution. Not properly classified as monotheism, many elements of Akhenaten's religion preceded his reign, and he reworked the worship of the sun-god in a way that strengthened the king's own divinity and importance to his society. Modern interpretations of Akhenaten tend to reflect to a significant extent the surrounding ethos of the commentators themselves. Writing in the 1980s, one noted Amarna scholar, Donald Redford, adopted a more cynical view of the king: "For all that can be said in his favor, Akhenaten in spirit remains to the end totalitarian. The right of the individual freely to choose was wholly foreign to him…I cannot conceive a more tiresome regime under which to be fated to live."

Was Akhenaten a king who genuinely strove to comprehend the nature of creation and his own relevance to his world, even as he grappled with the exigencies of rulership? In view of the poetic and effusive language of the *Hymn to the Aten*, it is hard to avoid the conclusion that Akhenaten was, indeed, an individual inspired and moved by the beauty of creation. Over 3,000 years later it is difficult to ascertain what his personality might have been like, but the modern rediscovery of Egypt's Amarna era has largely been driven by the enduring fascination of deciphering his mysterious persona.

FURTHER READING

Aldred, Cyril.
1957   "The End of the El- 'Amarna Period'." *Journal of Egyptian Archaeology* 3:33–41.
1971   *Jewels of the Pharaohs.* New York: Praeger.
1973   *Akhenaten and Nefertiti.* New York: Brooklyn Museum.
1976   "The Horizon of the Aten." *Journal of Egyptian Archaeology* 62:184.
1982   "El-Amarna." In *Excavating in Egypt: The Egypt Exploration Society 1882-1982*, edited by T. G. H. James, pp. 86–106. Chicago, IL: University of Chicago Press.
1988   *Akhenaten, King of Egypt.* New York: Thames & Hudson.

Aldred, Cyril, and A. T. Sandison.
1962   "The Pharaoh Akhenaten: A Problem in Egyptology and Pathology." *Bulletin of the History of Medicine* 36(6):293–316.

Allen, James P.
1989   "The Natural Philosophy of Akhenaten." In *Religion and Philosophy in Ancient Egypt*, Yale Egyptological Studies 3, edited by William Kelly Simpson, pp. 89–102. New Haven, CT: Yale University Press.
1991   "Akhenaten's 'Mystery' Coregent and Successor." *Amarna Letters* I, Essays on Ancient Egypt Series, edited by Dennis Forbes, pp. 74–85. San Francisco, CA: KMT Communications.
1994   "Nefertiti and Smenkh-ka-re." *Göttinger Miszellen* 141:7–17.
1996   "The Religion of Amarna." In *The Royal Women of Amarna: Images of Beauty from Ancient Egypt*, by Dorothea Arnold, pp. 3–5. New York: Metropolitan Museum of Art.
Forthcoming "The Amarna Succession." In *Causing His Name to Live: Studies in Egyptian Epigraphy and History in Memory of William J. Murnane*, edited by Peter J. Brand and Jacob Van Dijk. Amsterdam: Brill.

Anthes, Rudolf.
1954   *The Head of Queen Nofretete.* Berlin: Gebr. Mann Verlag.

Arnold, Dorothea.
1996   *The Royal Women of Amarna: Images of Beauty from Ancient Egypt.* New York: Metropolitan Museum of Art.

Assmann, Jan.
1975   "Aton." *Lexikon der Ägyptologie* 1:526–40.
1995   *Egyptian Solar Religion in the New Kingdom: Re, Amun and the Crisis of Polytheism*, translated by Anthony Alcock. New York: Kegan Paul.

Baikie, James.
2004   *The Amarna Age: A Study of the Crisis of the Ancient World.* New York: Columbia University Press.
2000   *Amarna Diplomacy: The Beginnings of International Relations.* Baltimore, MD: Johns Hopkins University Press.

Baines, John.
1998   "The Dawn of the Amarna Age." In *Amenhotep III: Perspectives on His Reign*, edited by David O'Connor and Eric H. Cline, pp. 271–312. Ann Arbor, MI: University of Michigan Press.

Bennett, John.
1939   "The Restoration Stela of Tutankhamun." *Journal of Egyptian Archaeology* 25:8–15.

Berman, Lawrence M., ed.
1990.   *The Art of Amenhotep II: Art Historical Analysis. Papers Presented at the International Symposium Held at the Cleveland Museum of Art, Cleveland, Ohio 20-21 November 1987.* Cleveland, OH: Cleveland Museum of Art.

Blackenberg-Van Delden, C.
1969   *The Large Commemorative Scarabs of Amenhotep III.* Leiden: Brill.

Boyce, Andrew.
1995   "Collar and Necklace Designs at Amarna: A Preliminary Study of Faience Pendants. In *Amarna Reports* VI, edited by Barry J. Kemp, pp. 336–71. London: Egypt Exploration Society.

Burridge, Alwyn.
1993   "A Perspective on Akhenaten: Amarna Art, Evidence of a Genetic Disorder in the Royal Family of 18th Dynasty Egypt." *Journal of the Society for the Study of Egyptian Antiquities* 23.

Caminos, Richardo A.
1975   "Ei." *Lexikon der Ägyptologie* 1:526–40.

Carter, Howard.
1923-33 *The Tomb of Tut-ankh-Amen*. 3 vols. New York: Cassell.

Chubb, Mary.
1998   *Nefertiti Lived Here*. London: Libri.

Davies, Norman de Garis.
1903-08 *The Rock Tombs of El Amarna*. 6 vols. London: Egypt Exploration Society.
1921   "Mural Paintings in the City of Akhetaten." *Journal of Egyptian Archaeology* 7:1–7.
1923   "Akhenaten at Thebes." *Journal of Egyptian Archaeology* 9:132–52.
1929   "The Paintings of the Northern Palace." In *The Mural Painting of el-Amarneh*, edited by Henri Frankfort, pp. #58–71. London: Egypt Exploration Society.

Davis, Theodore M., with Edward Ayrton, George Daressy, E. Harold Jones, Gaston Maspero, and Grafton Elliot Smith.
1910   *The Tomb of Queen Tiyi: The Discovery of the Tomb*. London: Constable; rpt. London: Duckworth, 2001.

Davis, Theodore M., with Lancelot Crane, George Daressy, and Gaston Maspero.
1912   *The Tombs of Harmhabi and Touatânkhamanou*. London: Constable.

Davis, Theodore M., with Howard Carter, Percy E. Newberry, and Gaston Maspero.
1907   *The Tomb of Iouya and Touiyou*. London: Constable.

Dobson, Aidan.
1990   "Crown Prince Djhutmose and the Royal Sons of the Eighteenth Dynasty." *Journal of Egyptian Archaeology* 76:87–96.

Eaton-Krauss, Marianne.
1985   "Tutanchamun." *Lexikon der Ägyptologie* 6:812–16.

Edwards, I. E. S.
1972   *Treasures of Tutankhamun*. New York: Viking Press.

Fairman, Herbert.
1972   "Tutankhamun and the End of the Eighteenth Dynasty." *Antiquity* 46:15–18.

Fay, Biri.
1986   "Nefertiti Times Three." *Jahrbuch der Berliner Museen* 23:359–76.

Frankfort, Henri, and J. D. S Pendlebury.
1933   *The City of Akhenaten* 2. London: Egypt Exploration Society.

Freed, Rita E., with Edward Brovarski and Susan K. Doll.
1982   *Egypt's Golden Age: The Art of the New Kingdom 1558-1085 B.C.* Boston, MA: Museum of Fine Arts, Boston.

Freed, Rita E., with Yvonne J. Markowitz and Sue H. D'Auria, eds.
1999   *Pharaohs of the Sun: Akhenaten, Nefertiti, Tutankhamun*. Boston, MA: Museum of Fine Arts, Boston.

Friedman, Florence, ed.
1998   *Gifts of the Nile: Ancient Egyptian Faience*. London and Providence, RI: hames & Hudson and Museum of the Rhode Island School of Design.

Giles, F. J.
1972   *Ikhnaton: Legend and History*. Rutherford, NJ: Fairleigh Dickinson University Press.

Gohary, Jocelyn.
1992   *Akhenaten's Sed-festival at Karnak*. New York: Kegan Paul.

Green, L.
1990   "A 'Lost Queen' of Ancient Egypt, King's Daughter, King's Great Wife, Ankhesenamen." *KMT: A Modern Journal of Ancient Egypt* 1(4):22–29.
1992   "Queen as Goddess: The Religious Role of Royal Women in the Late-Eighteenth Dynasty." *Amarna Letters* II, Essays on Ancient Egypt Series, edited by Dennis Forbes, pp. 28–41. San Francisco, CA: KMT Communications.

Griffith, Francis Llewellyn.
1918   "The Jubilee of Akhenaton." *Journal of Egyptian Archaeology* 5:61–63.
1926   "Stela in Honour of Amenophis III and Taya, from Tell el-`Amarnah." *Journal of Egyptian Archaeology* 12:1–2.

Gundlach, Rolf.
1986   "Taduhepa." *Lexikon der Ägyptologie* 6:526–40.

Hari, Robert.
1984   "La religion amarnienne et la tradition poythéiste." In *Studien zu Sprache und Religion Agyptens: zu Ehren von Wolfhart Westendorf* 2:1039–55. Göttingen: F. Junge.
1985   "Quelques remarques sur l'abandon d'Akhetaten." *Bulletin, Société d'Égyptologie* 9-10 (1984-85): 113–18.

Harris, John R. 1973 "Nefernefruaten." *Göttinger Miszellen* 4:15–17.
1974   "Kiya." *Chronique d'Égypte* 49:25–30.
1992   "Akhenaten and Nefernefruaten in the Tomb of Tu'ankhamun." In *After Tu'ankhamun: Research and Excavation in the Royal Necropolis at Thebes*, edited by Nicholas Reeves, pp. 55–72. London: Kegan Paul.

Hawass, Zahi.
1995   *Silent Images: Woman of Pharaonic Egypt.* Cairo: Ministry of Culture; rpt. New York: Harry Abrams, 2000.

Hayes, William C.
1951   "Inscriptions from the Palace of Amenhotep III." *Journal of Near Eastern Studies* 10:35–56, 56–111, 231–42.

Helck, Wolfgang.
1980   "Kija." *Lexikon der Ägyptologie* 3:422–24.
1984a   "Kijê." *Mitteilungen des Deutschen Archäologischen Instituts, Abteilung Kairo* 40:159–67.
1984b   "Meketaton." *Lexikon der Ägyptologie* 4:22–23.

Hornung, Erik.
1990   *Conception of God in Ancient Egypt: The One and the Many,* translated by John Baines. Ithaca, NY: Cornell University Press.
1992   "The Rediscovery of Akhenaten and His Place in Religion." *Journal of the American Research Center in Egypt* 29:43–49.
1995   *Echnaton. Die Religion des Lichtes.* Zurich: Artemis and Winkler.

Ikram, Salima.
1989   "Domestic Shrines and the Cult of the Royal Family at el-Amarna." *Journal of Egyptian Archaeology* 75:89–101.

James, T. G. H.
2000   *Tutankhamun: The Eternal Splendour of the Boy Pharaoh.* New York: Tauris Parke.

Janssen, Rosalind M., and Jac J. Janssen.
1990   *Growing Up in Ancient Egypt.* London: Rubicon.

Johnson, George B.
1991   "From What Material was Her Unique Regalia Constructed? Seeking Queen Nerfertiti's Tall Blue Crown: A Fifteen-Year Quest Ends in the Royal Tomb at el Amarna." *Amarna Letters* I. Essays on Ancient Egypt Series, edited by Dennis Forbes, pp. 50–61. San Francisco, CA: KMT Communications.

Johnson, W. Raymond.
1996   "Amenhotep III and Amarna: Some New Considerations." *Journal of Egyptology Archaeology* 82:65–82.

Kemp, Barry J.
1976   "The Window of Appearance at El-Amarna and the Basic Structure of this City." *Journal of Egyptian Archaeology* 62:81–99.
1977   "The City of El-Amarna as a Source from the Study of Urban Archaeology in Ancient Egypt." *World Archaeology* 9(2):123–39.
1979   "Wall Paintings from the Workmen's Village at el-Amarna." *Journal of Egyptian Archaeology* 65:47–53.

1981   "Preliminary Report on the El-Amarna Expedition 1980." *Journal of Egyptian Archaeology* 67:5–20.
1987   "The Amarna Workmen's Village in Retrospect." *Journal of Egyptian Archaeology* 73:21–50.
1989a   *Ancient Egypt: Anatomy of a Civilization.* New York: Routledge.
1989b   "Appendix: Workshops and Production at el-Amarna." In *Amarna Reports V,* edited by Barry J. Kemp, pp. 56–63. London: Egypt Exploration Fund.
1995   "Outlying Temples at Amarna." In *Amarna Reports* VI, edited by Barry J. Kemp, pp. 411–25. London: Egypt Exploration Fund.

Kemp, B., and S. Garfi.
1993   *A Survey of the Ancient City of Amarna.* London: Egypt Exploration Society.

Kitchen, K. A.
1962   *Suppuliuma and the Amarna Pharaohs: A Study in Relative Chronology.* Liverpool: Liverpool University Press.

Kozloff, Arielle P., with Betsy M. Bryan and Lawrence M. Berman.
1992   *Egypt's Dazzling Sun: Amenhotep III and His World.* Cleveland, OH: Cleveland Museum of Art.

Leprohon, Ronald J.
1991.   "A Vision Collapsed: Akhenaten's Reforms Viewed Through Decrees of Later Reigns." *Amarna Letters* I. Essays on Ancient Egypt Series, edited by Dennis Forbes, pp. 66-73. San Francisco, CA: KMT Communications.

Lloyd, Seton.
1933   "Model of a Tell el-Amarnah house." *Journal of Egyptian Archaeology* 19:1–7.

Loeben, Christian E.
1994a   "Nefertiti's Pillars: A Photo Essay of the Queen's Monument at Karnak." *Amarna Letters* III. Essays on Ancient Egypt Series, edited by Dennis Forbes, pp. 41–45. San Francisco, CA: KMT Communications.
1994b   "No Evidence of Coregency: Two Erased Inscriptions from Tutankhamen's Tomb." *Amarna Letters* III. Essays on Ancient Egypt Series, edited by Dennis Forbes, pp. 105–109. San Francisco, CA: KMT Communications.

Löhr, Beatrix.
1975   "Ahanjati in Memphis." *Studien zur altägyptischen Kultur* 2:139–87.

Martin, Geoffrey T.
1989a   *The Memphite Tomb of the Horemheb, Commander-in-Chief of Tutankhamun.* London: Egypt Exploration Society.

1989b   *The Royal Tomb of El-'Amarna*, vol. 2. London:
         Egypt Exploration Society.
1991   *A Bibliography of the Amarna Period and Its
         Aftermath: The reigns of Akhenaten, Smenkhkare,
         Tutankhamun, and Ay (c. 1350–13231 BC)*.
         New York: Kegan Paul.

Meltzer, Edmund S.
1978   "The Parentage of Tutankhamun and Smen-
         khkare." *Egyptian Archaeology* 64:134–35.

Mercer, Samuel A. B., with Frank Hudson Hallock.
1939   *The Tell el-Amarna Tablets*. 2 vols. Toronto:
         Macmillan.

Montserrat, Dominic.
2000   *Akhenaten. History, Fantasy and Ancient Egypt*.
         New York: Routledge.

Moran, William L., ed. and trans.
1992   *The Amarna Letters*. Baltimore, MD: Johns
         Hopkins University Press.

Morris, Ellen Fowles.
2005   *The Architecture of Imperialism: Military Bases
         and the Evolution of Foreign Policy in Egypt's New
         Kingdom*. Leiden: Brill.

Müller, Maya.
1988   *Die Kunst Amenophis' III. Und Echnatons*. Basel:
         Verlag für Ägyptologie.

Murnane, William J.
1995   *Texts from the Amarna Period in Egypt*. Writings
         from the Ancient World Series 5. Atlanta,
         GA: Society of Biblical Literature.

Murnane, William J., and Charles C. van Siclen III.
1993   *The Boundary Stelae of Akhenaten*. New York:
         Kegan Paul.

Nicholson, Paul T.
1993   *Egyptian Faience and Glass*. Princes Risbor-
         ough, Buckinghamshire, England: Shire
         Publications.

1995   "Glassmaking and Glassworking at Amarna:
         Some New Work." *Journal of Glass Studies*
         37:11–19.

Noblecourt, Christiane Desroches.
1963   *Tutankhamen: Life and Death of a Pharaoh*. New
         York: New York Graphic Society.

O'Connor, David B.
1988   "Demarcating the Boundaries: An Interpre-
         tation of Scene in the Tomb of Mahu at El-
         Amarna." *Bulletin of the Egyptological Seminar*
         9:41–52.
1989   "City and Palace in New Kingdom Egypt."
         *Cahier de Recherches de l'Institut de Papyrologie et
         d'Égyptologie de Lille* 11:73–87.

Peet. T. Eric.
1921   "Excavations at Tell el-Amarna." *Journal of
         Egyptian Archaeology* 7:169–85.

Peet, T. Eric, and C. Leonard Woolley.
1923   *The City of Akhenaten I*. London: Egypt Explo-
         ration Society.

Pendlebury, J. D. S.
1931   "Preliminary Report of Excavations at Tell
         El-'Amarnah, 1930-31." *Journal of Egyptian
         Archaeology* 17:233–44.

1935   *Tell el-Amarna*. London: L. Dickson & Thomp-
         son.

Pendlebury, J. D. S., with T. Eric Peet, C. Leonard
         Woolley, Battiscombe Gunn, and P. L. O.
         Guy.
1923   *The City of Akhenaten 3*. 2 vols. London: Egypt
         Exploration Society; rpt. 1972.

Petrie, W. M. F., with F. Ll. Griffith, A. H. Sayce, and
         F. C. J. Spurrell.
1894   *Tell el Amarna*. London: Methuen.

Phillips, Jacke.
1991   "Sculpture Ateliers of Akhetaten: An Exami-
         nation of Two Studio-Complexes in the City
         of the Sun-Disk." *Amarna Letters* I. Essays
         on Ancient Egypt Series, edited by Dennis
         Forbes, pp. 31–40. San Francisco, CA: KMT
         Communications.
1994   "The Composite Sculpture of Akhenaten:
         Some initial Thoughts and Questions."
         Amarna Letters III. Essays on Ancient Egypt
         Series, edited by Dennis Forbes, pp. 58–71.
         San Francisco, CA: KMT Communications.

Porter, Bertha, and Rosalind L. B. Moss.
1972   *Theban Temples. Pt. 2 of Topographical Bibliogra-
         phy of Ancient Egyptian Hieroglyphic Texts, Reliefs,
         and Paintings*. 2nd ed., rev. Oxford: Clarendon
         Press.

Redford, Donald B.
1973   "Studies on Akhenaten at Thebes I, A Re-
         port on the Work of the Akhenaten Temple
         Project of the University Museum, Uni-
         versity of Pennsylvania." *Journal of American
         Research Center in Egypt* 10:77–94.
1975   "Reconstructing the Temples of a Heretical
         Pharaoh." *Archaeology* 28:16–22.
1978   "The Razed Temple of Akhenaten." *Scientific
         American* 239(6):136–47.
1984   *Akhenaten: The Heretic King*. Princeton, NJ:
         Princeton University Press.
date?   *Pharaonic King-Lists, Annals and Day-Books*.
         Mississauga, ON, Canada: Benben.
1992   *Egypt, Canaan, and Israel in Ancient Times*.
         Princeton, NJ: Princeton University Press.

Reeves, C. Nicholas.
1990   *The Complete Tutankhamun: The King, The Tomb, The Real Treasure*. London: Thames & Hudson.

Reeves, C. Nicholas, and Richard H. Wilkinson.
1996   *The Complete Valley of the Kings*. London: Thames & Hudson.

Robins, Gay.
1992   "The Mother of Tutankhamun (2)." *Discussions in Egyptology* 22:25–27.
1993   "The Representations of Sexual Characteristics in Amarna Art." *Journal of the Society for the Study of Egyptian Antiquities* 23:29–41.

Roeder, Günther.
1969   *Amarna Reliefs aus Hermopolis*. Hildesheim: Gerstenberg.

Russmann, Edna R.
1989   *Egyptian Sculpture: Cairo and Luxor*. Austin, TX: University of Texas Press.

Saleh, Mohamed, and Hourig Sourouzian.
1987   *The Egyptian Museum Cairo: Official Catalogue*. Mainz: von Zabern.

Samson, Julia.
1972   *Amarna, City of Akhenaten and Nefertiti: Key Pieces from the Petrie Collection*. London: Aris & Phillips.
1973   "Amarna Crowns and Wigs." *Journal of Egyptian Archaeology* 59:47–59.
1985   *Nefertiti and Cleopatra: Queen-monarchs of Ancient Egypt*. London: Rubicon Press.
1976   "Royal Names in Amarna History." *Chronique d'Égypte* 51:30-38.
1978   *Amarna, City of Akhenaten and Nefertiti: Nefertiti as Pharaoh*. Warminster: Aris & Phillips.

Sandman, Maj.
1938   *Texts from the Time of Akhenaten* Bibliotheca Aegyptiaca 8 (Brussels 1938), compiled by L. G. Leeuwenburg. Leiden: Brill.

Schulman, Alan R.
1964   "Some Observations on the Military Background of the Amarna Period." *Journal of the American Research Center in Egypt* 3:51–69.

Shaw, Ian
1994a   "Balustrades, Stairs and Altars in the Cult of the Aten at el-Amarna." *Journal of Egyptian Archaeology* 80:109–27.
1994b   "Ring Bezels at el-Amarna." *Amarna Reports* I, edited by Barry J. Kemp, pp. 124–32. London: Egypt Exploration Society.

Silverman, David P.
1991a   "Divinities and Deities in Ancient Egypt." In *Religion in Ancient Egypt*, edited by Byron E. Shafer, pp. 8–87. Ithaca, NY: Cornell University Press.
1991b   "Texts from the Amarna Period and Their Position in the Development of Ancient Egyptian." *Lingua Aegyptica* 1:301-14.
1991c   "The So-Called Portal Temple of Ramesses II at Thebes." In *Akten des Vierten Internationalen Ägyptologen Kongresses München 1985*, edited by SylviSchoske, pp. 269-77. Hamburg: Helmut Buske.
1995   "The Nature of Egyptian Kingship." In *Ancient Egyptian Kingship*, edited by David O'Connor and David P. Silverman, pp. 49–94. Leiden: Brill.
1999   "A Litany from the Eighteenth Dynasty Tomb of Merneith." In *Gold of Praise: Studies on Ancient Egypt in Honor of Edward F. Wente*. Studies in Ancient Oriental Civilization 58, edited by Emily Teeter and John A. Larson, pp. 379-86. Chicago, IL: Oriental Institute.

Silverman, David P., ed.
1997   *Ancient Egypt*.New York: Oxford University Press.

Shortland, Andrew J.
2000   *Vitreous Materials at Amarna: The Production of Glass and Faience in the 18ᵗʰ Dynasty Egypt*. Oxford: BAR Archaeopress.

Smith, Ray W., and Donald B. Redford.
1976   *The Akhenaten Temple Project I: Initial Discoveries*. Warminster: Aris & Phillips.

Spence, Kate.
2004   "The Three-dimensional Form of the Amarna House." *Journal of Egyptian Archaeology* 90:123-52.

Thomas, Angela P.
1994   "The Other Woman at Akhetaten, Royal Wife Kiya." *Amarna Letters* III. Essays on Ancient Egypt Series, edited by Dennis Forbes, pp. 73–81. San Francisco, CA: KMT Communications.

Vergote, Jean.
1961   *Toutankhamon dans les archives Hittites*. Istanbul: Nederlands Historisch-Archeologisch Instituut in het Nabije Oosten.

Watterson, Barbara.
1999   *Amarna: Ancient Egypt's Age of Revolution*. Charleston, SC: Tempus.

Index